T0123798

When Did I Start Looking Like a Cop?

When Did I Start Looking Like a Cop?

JOSEPH BELCASTRO

iUniverse

WHEN DID I START LOOKING LIKE A COP?

iUniverse books may be ordered through booksellers or by contacting:

iUniverse
1663 Liberty Drive
Bloomington, IN 47403
www.iuniverse.com
1-800-Authors (1-800-288-4677)

Because of the dynamic nature of the Internet, any web addresses or links contained in this book may have changed since publication and may no longer be valid. The views expressed in this work are solely those of the author and do not necessarily reflect the views of the publisher, and the publisher hereby disclaims any responsibility for them.

Any people depicted in stock imagery provided by Thinkstock are models, and such images are being used for illustrative purposes only. Certain stock imagery © Thinkstock.

ISBN: 978-1-5320-0901-3 (sc)
ISBN: 978-1-5320-0900-6 (e)

Library of Congress Control Number: 2016918189

Print information available on the last page.

iUniverse rev. date: 11/02/2016

CONTENTS

PREFACE

Pure instinct is what transformed me from civilian to cop—forever. There was no going back.

I was a New York City police officer from July 1983 until July 2003. What follows is a compilation of short stories chosen from my twenty-year career policing the streets of some of the most dangerous precincts across the five boroughs of New York City. These stories provide an inside look into proactive policing in the eighties and nineties—a sampling, if you will, of what it was like to be a cop back then.

I will take you deep into the night, while most people were sleeping. Whether I was in uniform or plainclothes, my partners and I were out there, night after night, looking for the people who were looking to do harm to other people— bad guys out to destroy innocent lives and those of their families.

Not unlike hunters, we relied heavily on our instincts, watching and waiting. Observant, methodical, persistent, and determined, we got results, or we didn't go home.

I suspect that there will never be another unit quite like the Street Crime Unit. The days of following, searching, and investigating suspects based on our training, experience, and gut instinct seem to be long gone. I am so grateful to have worked during a time when we were empowered to make a real difference. And live to write about it.

1

ABOUT ME

My name is Joseph Belcastro. I was born in Brooklyn, New York, in the summer of 1956. My father was a longshoreman (like Marlon Brando's character in *On the Waterfront*)—guys who take the stuff off the ship but never take a trip on it. We didn't have a car back then, so he used to take the bus and train to work, always with that hook hanging over his shoulder. My mother was a typist in this huge room with about fifty other women typists (I think that's called a "typing pool".) She worked in Brooklyn on Eighty-Sixth Street under the L train. I had an older brother and a younger sister.

We lived in the Dyker Heights section with all the rest of the Italians. I grew up playing in the streets: hide-and-go-seek, ring-a-levio, stickball, slap ball, scully, and army. We flipped baseball cards and played colors. We'd roller-skate with those metal skates that would clamp onto the outside of our shoes using skate keys. The neighborhood kids would form teams and play baseball in the summer and football in the winter. All I ever wanted was to be a baseball player and to play with the New York Yankees, of course. When I was around eight years old, my mother took me to the optometrist, who told her that I needed glasses. Man, that was like the worst day of my life! I used to keep them hidden in my pocket and only put them on when absolutely necessary. I was so ashamed I had to wear them when none of my friends did.

Things were tough for us growing up. We lived in a small apartment. Our furniture consisted of lawn chairs, cast-off hassocks, folding beds, and a kitchen table. By 1968 we were able to move to Staten Island; we bought a house with my great-aunt (on my mother's side) and settled into Sunnyside. We lasted only two years there. My great-aunt turned out to be just one of a fast-growing group of people my father just couldn't get along with, so we were forced to sell. We relocated to the Fort Wadsworth section of Staten Island, but now I was pretty far from where I had been attending high school, and it was taking me forever to get there and back every day. I got lucky in my senior year when my father brought home a used Gremlin for my mother to drive. She refused to even get behind the wheel, so I had a car I could use to drive myself to school every day.

I played baseball in high school but wasn't good enough to get a scholarship, and my parents couldn't afford to send me to college without one. There weren't many options available to me back then, so I enlisted in the Marine Corps. Those two years would end up being the catalyst for everything that would come later on. But by the time I was (honorably) discharged, I still didn't know what I wanted to do with my life. I took a job as a security guard at a local hospital in Staten Island. I soon realized that was going nowhere; I suppose I could've taken advantage of the GI Bill and gone to college, but that wasn't where my head was at the time. I had taken a couple of city and state law enforcement civil service exams, and the first one to call was a New York State correction officer. Both my buddy Les and I passed the test, and I talked him into taking the job with me.

We wound up relocating to Upstate New York to be closer to the prison we were assigned to, but after a year, I'd had enough. My girlfriend (who later became my wife) had dreams of moving to Florida to open a business of our own, so I left Les and the Department of Corrections behind and moved south. I worked for a furniture store delivering furniture and then moved up to selling it. After about a year, we were able to buy a small beer-wine-and-soda store. It was going well for a while until the day Les came to visit ...

2

I GET THE NOD

For the past two years my wife and I had been living in Florida. I owned a small beer-wine-and-soda store, and we were doing okay. It seemed we had found our place and settled into what we thought life should be. If something was tugging at me, I wasn't able to put my finger on it. I was doing what I was supposed to be doing—making a life for me, my wife, and the family we would one day have.

We were expecting our first child when my one of my best friends, Les, came to Coral Springs to visit for the week. He had recently graduated from the New York Police Department Police Academy, and he loved it. Born and raised in New York City, becoming a NYC police officer had always been a dream of mine (right behind playing for the New York Yankees)—a dream my wife had successfully talked me out of several times. But now she watched my face as Les told me how excited he was to be a cop and talked about how if I came back to New York we could even be partners one day. She knew there was no talking me out of it this time.

Les left promising that he would check with the NYPD Applicant Investigation Unit to see if I was still eligible to be hired. Les telephoned a few days later and informed me that I was good to go. It meant selling my business in Florida, packing up, and moving back to New York City and finding a place to live—all on the chance that I would survive the background investigation and the physical, medical, and psychological testing that is part of the lengthy evaluation process a candidate endures before he or she can become a recruit. I was risking it all, but I also knew that to not take this chance would be to live a life of what could have been.

It was 1981. We traveled to New York and found an apartment in the Grymes Hill section of Staten Island. Then we went back to Florida, sold the business, rented a huge U-Haul truck, and packed it with all our belongings for the trip back north. At first I thought that now that I had made my decision, everything would just fall into place. As it turned out, a candidate is pretty much at the mercy of whoever you get as an investigator. Unfortunately for me, I had a new guy who really didn't know what he was doing. It looked like I was going to have to assist him as best I could in the process.

For two years I had to drive a livery cab and work for a moving company to support my family while my processing to become a NYPD police officer dragged on. But on that summer day in 1983 when I tore open the envelope notifying me that I had been accepted into the NYPD Police Academy, the two years of waiting had all but been forgotten. On July 25, 1983, everyone who received his or her acceptance notice had to report to the Fashion Institute of Technology (FIT) for orientation. I don't remember how big our academy class was, but we definitely filled the huge auditorium; there were about 1,500 recruits.

We had been sitting there for a while filling out tons of paperwork when an instructor came up to our section and asked us if there were any former military men in the group. A guy a couple of rows down from me shot his hand up like he wanted to be picked first. It turns out that in our group (which we would later refer to as our "company"), there were three prior military. The guy who couldn't wait to be picked (who turned out to be US Army) was named company sergeant. I (the US Marine) was named assistant company sergeant. And so the five months of training began.

3

COPS LIKE ME

There comes a time in most cops' careers when you either take a test for sergeant as a way to get promoted up through the ranks, or you request transfer to an investigative unit that could one day put you on the path to get your detective shield. I was never a good student and didn't like school, so I chose the path to the shield. I loved being on the street watching people, trying to figure out who the bad guys were.

There were those cops we called "Straight-Eights", "Empty Suits", or "Zeros"; they were the cops who would work their eight-and-a-half-hour tour and do as little as possible to collect a paycheck. They did not want anything to do with making arrests or working any overtime, and I didn't want anything to do with them. I wanted to work with guys like me who were totally motivated and who loved to be on the street making collars. These were the guys you could trust—the guys who knew how to talk to people. They had a way of talking to people, and asking the right questions was their best weapon. These were the guys who kept their eyes open and thought out loud: *What's this person doing? Let's watch this guy for a few minutes. Why did this guy do that? Let's stay with this car and see what's up.*

We kept information in our heads and remembered descriptions of persons wanted in connection with past crimes; we were the go-getters. We searched for the crime; we didn't wait for it to be in the past. We were known as cracker-jack cops who knew the streets. We got involved, knew what to look for, and never said "I'm 'not looking.'" In fact, we were *always* looking to make an arrest. Our tactics were sharp, our reflexes fast. Any time, any place, and we couldn't care less if the other cops resented us for it. We were out there doing the job and loving it. The overtime; the mounds of paperwork that came with processing every arrest; the mindless hours waiting to see the Assistant District Attorney (ADA); the court appearances; the forfeited family dinners, social gatherings, and holidays—it was all worth it, because we took a bad person off the street who had beaten or robbed some innocent person. It felt good, and it made other people feel safe.

Some cops get comfortable and stayed in one precinct their entire careers, but in the citywide unit I was assigned to, I got to work in every high-crime precinct in the city. It was a wild ride I never wanted to get off. I couldn't wait to get to work each day. I had great partners, and I will never forget them. We became a family—a family of warriors.

4

MY FIRS† Day

It was December 26, and I had to report to the NSU (Neighborhood Stabilization Unit) in the Seven-One Precinct. The night before, I had pressed my uniform shirt and pants with razor-sharp military creases. I had all my gear attached to my gun belt, my *Corfam* (patent-leather) shoes, my cap device on my cover (hat), my tie clasp—I was "AJ-squared away". I had one problem, though. My car was on the blink. So I reached out to my best friend Les and asked him if I could borrow his car since he was on his RDOs (regular days off). He dropped the car off to me that night, and I was good to go. I had called the Seven-One Precinct and asked for directions, because I had never been to the Crown Heights section of Brooklyn before. After that, I was all set.

The next morning came, and I did the three S's (shit, shower, and shave), put on my uniform, went outside, got in the car, turned the key, and nothing—not even a click. I couldn't believe it. My first day on the job, and even the car I borrowed wouldn't start. I was like, *What the fuck?!* So

I said to myself, *Let me go back to* my *car and see if it starts.* And—*boom*—wouldn't you know? It started. But by now I was panicking because I was going to be late for my first roll call.

I bolted out of the driveway, got down to the Staten Island Expressway, over the Verrazano Bridge to the Gowanus, and headed toward the Prospect Expressway. I got off at Eleventh Avenue, cut across to Prospect Park, drove through the park, headed down Empire Boulevard to New York Ave, and I was done—there. The only problem was I remembered the precinct cop who had given me the directions told me not to park in the precinct parking lot; it was reserved for the cops assigned to the Seven-One. But I was late and the streets were packed with parked cars, so I thought, *Fuck it. I'll just have to take a chance.* I pulled into the lot.

Gear in hand, I blasted through the back door of the precinct. Two cops immediately confronted me and asked where I was going. I explained that I was reporting for duty to NSU Twelve. They told me that I was late and that I was going to get a *command discipline* (written up for misconduct). Even though I was wearing a name plate under my shield, they asked me my name, and then one of them scribbled something on the clipboard he was holding. After a few seconds, he told me to report upstairs to the muster room. By then, I had developed a screaming headache besides feeling like an asshole for being late, because I was *never* late for anything.

Later on in the day I mentioned to some of the other cops what happened to me, and they started laughing hysterically. One cop said, "My brother, those were just two regular Seven-One cops busting your balls. They're not bosses; they're just like us."

Man, I couldn't believe I'd fallen for a rookie prank like that. Those guys had gotten me good. I spent the next six months in that precinct looking to run into them again, but I never did.

5

NSU

Newly graduated police officers were called rookies. Back in the day, the first command a rookie was assigned to out of the academy was called a *Neighborhood Stabilization Unit*, or *NSU*. The NSU consisted of four precincts. You would report to the same precinct each day for work, but you could be assigned to any of the other three precincts to work for that tour.

I was assigned to NSU Twelve, which was anything but stable. NSU Twelve operated out of the Seven-One Precinct in Crown Heights, Brooklyn, and covered four high-crime precincts: the Six-Three, Six-Seven, Six-Nine, and Seven-One Precincts. Most of the foot posts I was assigned to were in the Six-Seven Precinct. I found it pretty amazing that people in such a high-crime neighborhood would say good morning to me and tell me things like they were happy to see me there. I would stand out there on my assigned post and have my ear to the radio, hoping that I'd get a gun-run or some other heavy *job* (assignment over the radio from the central dispatcher) so I could spring into action. Half the time I didn't even know where the hell I was, but when it's a matter of survival, you learn quickly. The most important thing was to know your exact location at all times in case you had to call a "10-85 forthwith" (additional unit needed) or "10-13" (police officer needs assistance).

It didn't take me long to realize it was all for show—sticking a bunch of shiny new police officers on every corner as if we would be a big deterrent; meanwhile, the crime just moved indoors. People could tell we were brand-new—our alert posture, neat uniforms, stiff leather, and unblemished equipment gave us away. We passed our days dutifully standing at our foot posts and praying we didn't embarrass ourselves.

A gun-run would come over the radio, and I would acknowledge Central (the dispatcher), give them my post number, and tell them that I was responding, but they would instruct me to stand by and wait for the sector car to show. I discovered that this was because sometimes, like when cops were responding to a *housing location* (housing project), people would throw random things off the roof at the cops, like a couch or a chair. So we always had to stay sharp. We were in the shit now, and school was definitely out. We spent our six months in NSU just trying to get a feel for the streets, sometimes standing a foot post and sometimes riding in an RMP (radio motor patrol car). We were assigned to training detectives who were supposed to teach us how to respond to certain situations and how to interact with the public, but I never learned anything from them. It seemed for the most part like they just took the assignment to get steady hours with weekends off. That is not to say that they weren't some great training detectives out there, there just weren't any assigned where I was.

I got lucky with my NSU squad sergeant, though. He happened to be a great supervisor, someone I admired and respected and would run into again later in my career. I was assigned to drive him the night I made my first gun collar. It was the first medal I ever received. He was a sharp cop and became a lifelong friend.

6

NAKED (OF KNOWLEDGE) AND AFRAID

O n this particular day tour, I was assigned to a two-man foot post within the confines of the Six-Seven Precinct. A job from Central came over the air: report of an attempted GLA (grand larceny auto) in progress. My partner John advised Central that we would respond to the location to investigate.

As we approached the corner, we observed a male Hispanic putting lug nuts on the left-front tire of a vehicle. As we got closer I called out, "Yo, my man, what's up?"

With that, he jumped up, threw the tire iron at us, and took off. We gave chase and put it over the radio that we were in a foot pursuit, yelling our location and direction into the radio as we ran. Suddenly the guy jumped a fence, and—*boom*—we were right on him. We grabbed him and handcuffed him.

I said, "That's right, my brother. You can't run for shit!"

I radioed Central to have a sector car "85" us at our

location for transport back to the station house. I guess I forgot to say "10-85 *no emergency*," because these precinct cops came with lights and sirens, thinking that we were in trouble. When they arrived and saw we were new on the job, they didn't criticize us for our mistake. We picked up our prisoner, put him in the back of the radio car, and off we went to the Six-Seven Precinct.

We brought our prisoner in front of the lieutenant at the desk who advised us to make sure he didn't have any weapons or drugs on him before we put him in a holding cell. And that was it. No other instruction or direction whatsoever. *What were we supposed to do once we lodged our prisoner in the cell? What paperwork did we need to fill out, and where was it located? What did we do with the stolen car? Who was going to fingerprint our prisoner?* It was like we had suddenly found ourselves naked and afraid. My head was spinning.

All of a sudden, this older veteran cop appeared out of nowhere—jet-black hair, uniform tie undone, and a rack of medals above his shield that extended up over his shoulder. He had an air of confidence, like he knew everything there was to know about processing an arrest and all the paperwork that came with it. He asked us what we had. So while John was trying to figure out how to fingerprint our prisoner, I told this cop about our collar. He started handing me forms to complete, telling me, "You need this, get rid of that, call here, notify this unit, cancel this …"

Before we knew it, we were back in front of the desk lieutenant with all our paperwork squared away, our prisoner printed, the vehicle alarm cancelled, and vouchers properly completed. We had everything we needed to bring him to Brooklyn Central Booking (BCB) and then to the DA's (district attorney's) office to draw up the complaint against him. When we were all done, we went back to the Seven-One Precinct to sign out, and I remember thinking, *Someday I'm going to be that cop—the cop everyone comes to with all the questions—and it will be me who gives them all the answers.*

7

OFF-DUTY COLLAR (NOT)

John and I used to carpool to the Seven-One Precinct every day. We had just finished a day tour and were on our way back to Staten Island. We were stopped at a light by the entrance to the Gowanus Expressway when I looked to my right and saw a guy in the car next to us looking at a handgun.

I told John, "Look to your right … That guy has a gun!"

Here we were: two off-duty rookie cops and we needed to take police action. The light turned green, and we got behind the guy as he entered the expressway. We stayed right behind him; the traffic was bumper-to-bumper like it always was at rush hour in New York City, but just then we saw a Highway Patrol car up ahead, handling a vehicle accident. We continued our crawl behind the guy who, of course, had no idea who we were or even that we were following him. Meanwhile, we were frantically trying to devise a plan on how we would stop him. The traffic came to an abrupt halt, so I told John I was going to run up ahead to the highway cops to tell them what we had. With that, I jumped out of the car, jogged up to the highway unit, identified myself as an off-duty police officer, and told him what we had just seen.

The highway cops signaled to the slow-moving traffic, bringing it to a complete stop. I joined them as they walked back to where the car was stopped behind a tractor-trailer. Because of the huge truck in the way, the driver didn't see us until the last second. When we got to the trailer's rear, we could see other motorists looking at us and probably saying to themselves, *What the hell are these cops doing now?* As we came into view of the guy with the gun, John jumped out of his car. All of us—the two highway cops in uniform and John and I in our civilian clothes—converged on the guy's vehicle with our guns drawn.

"Let me see your hands!" we shouted at him. "Where's the gun?"

We pulled him from the vehicle and threw him down to the ground, and all the while he's yelling in Russian-accented English, "It is starter's pistol! It is starter's pistol!"

After he was handcuffed, one of us finally realized what he had been saying: *It was a starter's pistol,* meaning a gun used at track meets. We all looked at each other like *holy shit,* but we couldn't have known that for sure until we got him out of the car and recovered the gun. The highway cops transported our prisoner to the Seven-Two Precinct on Fourth Avenue, which is where we had to go to process the arrest. Because we were off-duty, the precinct desk officer would have to notify the duty captain, and there would be a shitload of extra paperwork along with all kinds of notifications that would have to be made. They were not going to be happy with us.

The desk officer took one look at us and said, "What is this shit?" And I kind of knew what was coming. The lieutenant was not happy about the prospect of dealing with the shit-storm of paperwork and notifications that were sure to make his day miserable from start to finish. He continued to glare at me as I calmly explained what had happened.

The boss looked down from the desk at us and spoke slowly and purposefully. "This is what we are going to do. You are going to run his name to see if he has any warrants. If he doesn't have any warrants, you are going to issue him a *summons* for possession of an *imitation pistol* and send him on his way. Is that understood?"

As it turned out, the firearm in question actually *was* a starter's pistol (or what the New York State Penal Law defines as an "imitation pistol"), and possession of an imitation pistol *can* be a summonsable offense. Technically, if a summons were to be issued *in lieu of* arrest, then the entire incident would not be considered an *off-duty arrest*; therefore, the duty captain wouldn't have to be called, and no notifications or extra paperwork would have to completed.

"Is that understood?" the lieutenant repeated, impatient for me to get his point.

"Aye-aye, sir," I answered for my only off-duty (almost) arrest.

8

THE VILLAGE CONSTABLE

The six months in NSU had flown by, and I was finally transferred to my permanent command, the Sixth Precinct. I'd never heard of the Sixth Precinct; I had no idea where it was. At first I thought they meant the *Sixty-Sixth Precinct* (which is in the middle of a Hasidic neighborhood in Brooklyn with no action at all), but they kept saying the *Sixth*. I soon found out that the Sixth Precinct was in downtown Manhattan on the west side. I reported for duty on June 24, 1984.

The Sixth Precinct covered the West Village, also known as Greenwich Village. It encompassed the west side of Broadway, from West Fourteenth Street to West Houston Street, all the way down to the West Side Highway.

Every precinct throughout New York City is divided into patrol sectors that are assigned letter designations. In the Sixth Precinct, the sectors were labeled *A* through *I* and were often combined to form a single sector car's assignment for the tour. In the Sixth Precinct, the day tour (8:00 a.m. to 4:00 p.m.) and the four-to-twelve (4:00 p.m. to midnight) shifts usually turned out the most sector cars (four or five). On a midnight, which was a midnight-to-eight tour, it was, as a rule, less busy, and generally three sector cars would patrol the entire precinct.

A typical day tour might have Sectors A-B, C-D, E-F, and G-H-I (four patrol cars), plus a patrol supervisor. The four-to-twelve would have Sector A-B, C-D, E, F-G, and H-I (five patrol cars) and maybe two patrol supervisors. Whereas the midnight, when there were usually fewer calls for service, could turn out just three sectors cars: Sectors A-B-C, D-E-F, and G-H-I, with, of course, a patrol supervisor. These decisions were made by the desk officer for that tour, as he or she adjusted the roll call and sorted out manpower, vehicle availability, and minimum manning requirements.

In addition to sector cars, police officers, usually rookies or those with less seniority, would be assigned to foot posts throughout the precinct, usually in areas that saw a lot of pedestrian and tourist activity. As a general rule, a cop wouldn't be assigned a foot post on a midnight, unless he or she really pissed somebody off.

One of things that made the Village unique is that its streets were off the grid—they were set at an angle to the other streets in Manhattan. West Fourth Street crossed West Tenth, West Eleventh and West Twelfth Streets, ending at an intersection with West Thirteenth Street. Heading north on Greenwich Street, West Twelfth Street was separated by three blocks from Little West Twelfth Street, which, in turn, was one block south of West Thirteenth Street. There was Greenwich Avenue and Greenwich Street; Washington Square North, South, East, and West and Washington

Street; Eighth Avenue and Eighth Street. Street names changed when they converged at Washington Square Park and reverted back once you passed the park. There were tiny, hidden enclaves like Minetta Street and Commerce Lane. All this uniqueness, while charming, would make it a little harder for cops newly assigned to the precinct to find their way around.

The Village was as renowned for its artistic, Bohemian residents as it was for its quaint cafés, historic brownstones, and six-story walk-ups; some of the streets were still made of cobblestone. There was no bad area in the precinct—no low-income housing or housing projects. The average criminal could not afford to live in the West Village. They came in from other parts of the city to commit their crimes and then ducked into the nearest subway to escape.

In order to preserve the area's unique characteristics, many of the buildings in the West Village were historically protected from any renovations that would change the appearance of their existing facades. Ornate, beveled, lead glass entryway doors, while aesthetically more appealing than tempered glass and steel, would not prove much of a deterrent to a resourceful homeless person in search of a warm vestibule or hallway to shelter in on a cold night. Then there was always the more ambitious type of intruder—the kind who would take it a step further and break into an apartment in search of valuables. They would even, possibly, lie in wait around a bend in a hallway to ambush an unsuspecting tenant as they hurried in from the elements.

In the early 1900s, the west side of the precinct was predominantly commercial rather than residential, but gentrification had many of the old factories converted to large apartment buildings with artists' lofts. Still, there remained an expanse of undeveloped property in the confines of the Sixth Precinct that separated the West Side Highway and the Hudson River. This wide-open area, known to the cops in the Sixth simply as *The Pier*, was unpaved, with loose gravel covering the ground right up to the water's edge. Randomly placed railroad ties were the only thing preventing a car from plummeting over the edge and into the river. At night, the area became the clandestine gathering place for same-sex hookups, transvestite prostitutes, and drug deals.

The Sixth Precinct's jurisdiction over this tract of land ended at West Fourteenth Street. There was a large Department of Sanitation storage facility on the pier at Gansevoort Street where, no matter what the season, a mountain of street salt could be seen from the street, spilling out of the open warehouse. Homeless people were known to gather in shadows and protection of the building, disturbed only when cops were summoned to rouse them. Cops in the precinct referred to this illicit homeless haven as *The Salt Mines*.

The Meat Market, home to meat-packing businesses from Gansevoort Street to West Fourteenth Street, would get their start around four o'clock in the morning, just when most of the restaurants and bars in the area would be closing their doors for the night. Transvestite prostitutes avoided cops' attention by dodging in between the idling refrigerated tractor-trailers, as sides of beef were unloaded into the processing plants.

The Sixth Precinct station house itself was on West Tenth Street between Bleecker and Hudson streets. I couldn't believe how cool this place was, tucked into the block so tight you'd miss it if you drove by too fast. The front driveway of the station house parking lot exited onto Tenth Street and the back driveway onto Charles Street, where they say the original Sixth Precinct used to be back in the day. It was surrounded by residential brownstones, small boutiques, and intimate cafés.

Streets throughout the Village were always packed with people walking around, residents and tourists alike. One day, while I was standing on a foot post on Seventh Avenue, I heard someone calling out, "Constable, constable!" in a British accent. I looked all around before I realized he was talking to me.

I was one of fifteen newly assigned rookie cops, fresh out of different NSUs around the city. We all stood in the muster room of the precinct, waiting for roll call. I immediately singled out a big, tall Irish kid named Pete. He was full of tattoos, but one in particular caught my eye—the USMC insignia. He was a former Marine like me. After talking to Pete, I learned he had graduated from the Police Academy with the second-highest academic average of the whole class, but that didn't stop me from asking him if he wanted to work with me. We partnered up, and after a couple of weeks on foot posts, we finally started getting assigned to a sector car together. Pete and I worked so well together that we teamed up for a lot of off-duty gigs, too. We always had a lot of laughs, but after about a year and half, Pete put in for *CPOP* (Community Police Officer Program), which was a new detail within the precinct, and that left me without a partner again.

Les, one of my best friends growing up in Staten Island, was assigned to a nearby precinct, the First Precinct on

Varick Street. Les and I had had gone through junior high and high school together, played football and baseball on the same teams, and remained close friends even after we graduated. After we became cops, we would go out after work, talk shop, and swap war stories. So I asked Les if he would consider transferring over to the Sixth so we could partner up. As it happened, Les had a connection higher up in the department (what we cops refer to as a *hook*), so it didn't take long for Les' transfer to come through and for us to be assigned as partners in a steady sector in the Sixth Precinct.

It was kind of cool working with my best friend; we had the same way of thinking. As soon as we started working together, we began making a ton of arrests, from *car boosters* (people breaking into parked cars to steal the contents) to *GLAs* (grand larceny autos) to grand larcenies, robberies, and burglaries. We were always out there looking for an arrest. Even though we were pretty successful, we still felt like there was something holding us back. After all, we were in uniform and tied to a radio. We had tried to overcome that obstacle by bringing civilian jackets with us out on patrol to put over our uniforms. That way, when we wanted to follow someone we thought *looked good* (ready to commit a crime), we could use the jackets to hide our uniforms and follow them on foot without them realizing we were cops. Most times, Les would stay behind in the car and monitor the radio while I followed them.

One night, we were actually able to make four different *observation arrests*. An observation arrest is when a police officer observes an individual actually committing a crime in-progress, as opposed to waiting to get a radio run from Central about a crime that occurred in the past. This was almost unheard of for uniform cops on patrol, because the uniform and the marked police car announced our presence. But our eyes were always on the street. We would go through a checklist of reasonable explanations for an individual's presence at a certain location at a certain time. We would watch to see whether they changed direction back and forth. If their behavior did not seem reasonable to us, then they were worth following to see what developed.

While Les and I were on patrol one day, a woman stopped us and said, "I think that these two guys are trying to pickpocket people." She pointed to them, and sure enough, they were changing direction. We realized we might have something. We devised a plan to follow them, even though we were in uniform in a marked radio car. I got out of the car while Les headed back to the precinct to sign out a second radio; back in the day, each radio car team was only assigned one radio.

The Village was packed with people as usual, but *picks* (pickpockets) are really slick, and they don't care if there is a police car sitting there or a foot cop on the post right near them. They think that they are *that good* and that a cop wouldn't be able to make them as picks. But as soon as they passed this one lady going the opposite direction, I saw them turn to follow her, and I knew I had them. My only problem was that I was in full uniform, ducking in and out of stores, with people coming up to me and asking me questions. All the while I am trying to stay hidden from the picks and make sure I didn't lose them.

The two picks continued to follow the woman for a block or so until she went to enter a *Teamo* Smoke Shop and that's when they finally made their move. One of guys cut in front of the woman, stopping short. She bumped into him, and the guy behind her opened her pocketbook and removed her wallet. I couldn't believe I saw the whole thing go down, and the lady didn't feel a thing. The lady and the two guys then continued into the smoke shop together. I ran toward the store, figuring that they were still in there and couldn't go anywhere. But just as I was about to reach the store, the perp who had removed the woman's wallet came out. He looked right at me and took off.

Luckily, I was only ten feet behind him, but I didn't have time to put the pursuit over the radio to let Les know what was going on. As I grabbed the guy, a bystander who saw what happened stepped in to help me take the guy to the ground. I heard the sound of tires screeching as Les brought the radio car to a sudden stop in front of us.

"Joey!" he yelled, "You couldn't fuck wait for me?"

BLUES IN THE NIGHT

Lynn Snowden keeps the beat
with New York's finest

photograph by CHIP SIMONS

9

THEY CALL ME BELLHOP

One freezing-cold night early on in my career, I was assigned to a foot post on the west side of the Sixth Precinct. I was walking up and down Bleecker Street, trying to stay warm and look like I knew what I was doing. The sergeant on patrol for that tour would come around to give you a scratch (sign your memo book) at some point during the tour just to make sure you were where you were supposed to be. I listened attentively to the radio for my post number to be called.

I had never met this sergeant before, so I didn't know what to expect when suddenly I heard "Six Sergeant" ask Central to raise my post number (ascertain my location). I quickly acknowledged by responding to the dispatcher with my location. Within minutes, the sergeant's RMP rolled up. I walked over to the passenger side of the car and saluted the sergeant, but not before I thought to myself, *Holy shit! It's Burgess Meredith,* because that is exactly who the sergeant looked like.

Well, the sergeant did not return my salute. And

before I could even read the name etched on the gold plate beneath his shield, he grabbed my memo book with one hand and reached out to touch my shield with the other. I was like, *What the hell?* But then I realized he was checking to see if my shield, which was pinned to the outside of my duty jacket, was, in fact, cold. If it was, then it was proof that I had been out there, walking my post. If it wasn't, then I must have been inside somewhere, ducking the cold. I didn't know this sergeant, but instinct told me I did not want to be the foot cop he caught with the room-temperature shield on a frigid night.

The sergeant starting asking me questions like what NSU I came from and how long I had on the job. He asked me if I had been in the military, to which I proudly replied, "Yes, sir, the Marines." The rest of our brief conversation went something like this:

The sergeant: "All Marines are seagoing bellhops!"

Me (caught off guard): "What?"

The sergeant: "All they do is run errands aboard Navy ships and pull brig duty."

Me (defensive): "Were *you* in the service?"

The sergeant (proudly): "Yeah, the US Army."

Me: "In what, the Calvary"?

To which he just grumbled some Burgess Meredith–like shit and told his driver to go. And so it was that ever since that night, I was tagged with the nickname *Bellhop*. Anytime anyone was calling me on the police radio, they would say, "Hey, Bellhop, you on the air?" That nickname stuck to me throughout the rest of my career.

I often think of Sergeant O'Donnell, especially the day he passed away. We stood at attention in our dress blues on a blustery cold day in front of the church, right arms locked up in a salute. As they played taps, I wept and recalled how he gave me that nickname that still follows me today. I will never forget you, Sarge. *Bellhop.*

10

HaRD tO MaKE

There were people out there committing crimes who were hard to catch. The most obvious reason for this was that we were wearing uniforms, and the bad guys could see us coming a mile away. In the Sixth Precinct, weed dealers and three-card monte street hustlers were out of control. Pot dealers were big around Washington Square Park where all the NYU college kids and tourists were tripping over each other.

One strategy we came up with was for one of us to take an *OP*. An *OP* was an observation post; a hidden position from where we could to watch these guys and identify the players. We would hide someplace long enough to figure out who the dealers and buyers were and where they hid their stash, observe them in a hand-to-hand transaction (sale), and then—*boom*—we got them. Then we'd notify the field team to move in and lock them up.

Three-card monte is a trick card game where three cards are shuffled facedown and you bet on guessing correctly where the queen is, except that you never can. It's rigged, and you lose all your money. In your typical three-card monte scam, there are usually three players: the dealer, the player, and the lookout (the lookout being the most important). Also with a typical three-card monte scam, you had to practically be invisible to catch the guys, so this required a unique plan.

Most of the three-card monte games in the Sixth Precinct went down on West Fourteenth Street between Fifth and Sixth avenues. We figured out a way to get up on the roof of one of the buildings on West Thirteenth Street. The view from there gave us the best chance of seeing all the players involved, and one of the things I'd already learned is that *no one ever looks up*. After we had all the players involved identified, we exited the building and calmly walked down the street toward them. We could hear the whistle go out, signaling that *five-o* was on the block, but by then, it didn't matter. We had them. They had thought they were so slick, so invincible—they couldn't believe we had figured out a way to get them.

What we did to catch these three-card monte guys may not have been quantum physics, but it worked. And while the crime itself was a misdemeanor, and misdemeanors normally qualified for a summons or desk appearance ticket (which meant no trip to jail; they would appear in court at a later date), three-card monte games had become so prevalent and so profitable and generated so many complaints from store owners and the victims who were getting ripped off, it had been classified as a *precinct condition*. This meant that, as an added deterrent, anyone locked up for a precinct condition would *go through the system* (Central Booking) and spend a night or two (or three) in jail.

Sometimes I netted as much as fifteen hours of overtime. So before you go thinking it was no big deal to lock these guys up for a "trick card game", tell that to the unsuspecting tourist or the person who thought they could make a quick buck by knowing where the queen was—and all the money they lost thinking they were smarter than the dealers. We may have succeeded in shutting them down at that location, but I am sure that when they finally got out of jail, they relocated and started up somewhere else. Just as I was sure that the people would be back, playing and trying to win some money, just not while I was on the street—or on the roof.

11

THE StaBBing VictiM

We received a job of a "10-30" (robbery-in-progress) in a deli down on the west side of the Village. My partner Pete and I responded lights-and-siren to the location. When we arrived, we found the complainant on the floor inside the deli, bleeding from a chest wound. We immediately called for a *bus* (ambulance) to respond. The guy was lying on his side, moaning from the pain, but I knew I had to ask him some questions. I asked him if he knew the person who'd done this to him and after several attempts to get him to respond, he finally told me he knew the guy. He gave us a description. I felt there was more to the story, but I was afraid he wasn't going to have time to tell it.

Another patrol car arrived on the scene and agreed to wait with the victim until the ambulance arrived, which freed up Pete and me to canvas the area to look for a guy who matched the description the victim had given us. After driving just a few blocks, I couldn't believe it—we spotted the guy. We jumped out and grabbed him. He still had the knife, which we took from him before bringing him back to the scene. The victim was critical and was being frantically worked on by the paramedics, but we still had to conduct a *show-up identification* to make sure we had the right guy. Normally with a show-up ID, you would bring the victim to where you first grabbed the perp, but because the complainant was critically injured, we had to make an exception. And—*bingo*—positive identification. It was hard on the victim—he had lost a lot of blood and was in a great deal of pain (we found out later he had a collapsed lung as a result of the stab wound) but he managed to pull through.

And so began the criminal justice process: interviewing witnesses, grand jury appearances and hearings, and possibly a trial (if the bad guy wasn't offered a plea deal). The wheels of the system turn very slowly, but if you do your job well enough, you may get to see justice prevail. Hopefully sooner rather than later.

12

LUCKED OUT

One night on a four-to-twelve tour, Les and I were on patrol when we got a pickup job (a job we got from the street, not from the dispatcher) of a "man with a gun". A woman flagged us down and told us that there was a "white or Spanish guy" around the corner near the elementary school. She said that he was bleeding and had a silver gun in his hand. We headed toward the location and sure enough, before we even got to the corner, a guy came walking around the block. He was bleeding from his head and had a gun in his hand. We stopped the car, jumped out, and positioned ourselves behind the RMP doors. We drew our service revolvers and yelled at the guy to drop his gun, but he just kept walking toward us as if he didn't hear us. After repeated demands for him to drop the gun, he slowly started to raise it. I could feel myself starting to depress the trigger of my own gun while thinking to myself, *Okay this is it. This guy's going to get shot.* All the conditions were in place; we would have been justified. But just as that last thought crossed my mind, the guy dropped his gun and hit the deck. *What a relief.*

We approached him, handcuffed him, recovered his gun, and brought him into the Sixth Precinct. We called a bus to get his head wound looked at and then sat down with him to wait and asked him what happened. He told us he had been jumped by some guy who beat him up and took his money, so he took it upon himself to go home, get his gun, and go in search of the guy "to scare him". Sounds like a plan, right? Except for the fact that (1) he was intoxicated, (2) he was an *auxiliary* police officer at the Sixth Precinct, and (3) it was a *fake* gun (imitation pistol). Now when you are a cop confronting someone who is *armed* (gun-in-hand), you don't know—you *can't know*—any of that. It is either *comply* or *die*. This stupid kid nearly *lost his life* that night because he wanted to find the guy who robbed him and get his revenge—his deluded version of street justice.

It might be hard for someone to look back on a night when they were beaten and robbed and then *locked up* and somehow still manage to consider it their *lucky night*, but for him, it turned out to be exactly that.

13

HiTCHiNG a RiDE

It was a summer night in Manhattan in 1985. I was sitting in my car working an off-duty gig to make some extra money when suddenly two guys bolted right past my car. At first I didn't think anything of it, but then I saw two *mounted cops* (on horseback) galloping up the block after them, followed by two cops on foot running in the same direction.

I jumped out of my car, identified myself as a police officer to the two cops on foot, and asked them what they had. They told me that two male blacks had just robbed a jewelry store. It was not known if they were armed (had weapons). I asked the cops if they had a clothing description of the males, and they described the exact clothing of the two guys who had just run past me. I told the cops the direction I saw the guys run in and then joined in the chase. This all happened so fast; in a matter of a few seconds, we had spotted the two suspects. But when they realized we were chasing them, they split up. The two cops on foot went after one guy, and I went after the other. I was off-duty, in civilian clothes. I didn't have a radio. I had my five-shot off-duty revolver in my hand, and I was running through the streets of midtown Manhattan chasing a guy who had just robbed a jewelry store and may be armed—not the smartest thing I had ever done.

I am pretty fast, but I was not closing the gap between us when I saw a horse and carriage in the street—Hansom cabs were a favorite tourist attraction in and around Central Park. Before I even realized what I was doing, I jumped up onto the front of the carriage, identified myself as a police officer to the driver, and ordered him to chase the guy running down the street in front of us. I totally disregarded the five passengers in the carriage (no doubt tourists) who were yelling and screaming in absolute terror. They had no idea who I was or what I was doing; all they could see was a lunatic with a gun telling their carriage driver to go faster and all they knew was that their worst fears about big, bad New York City had finally come true before their very eyes. Oh, the stories they could tell when they got back home.

We actually started to catch up to the guy, so I ordered the driver to slow down (as if he had power brakes). He jerked back suddenly on the reins. The people in the carriage were huddled on top of one another, trying to stay as far from me as they could. I couldn't wait any longer; I put my foot on the step of the carriage and leapt off. But my foot caught on the carriage step, and I fell straight to the ground. The left-rear wheel of the carriage then rolled over my gun arm and sent my pistol flying across the street. The carriage continued up the block as if its journey had never been interrupted.

I crawled across the street to retrieve my pistol, but now

some bystanders thought I had been shot. I could hear sirens wailing in the distance. The two cops came running up with one of the perps in custody. Someone had called in a "10-13" (police officer needs assistance). A large crowd had formed, and I slowly backed my way into it, willing myself to blend in enough to disappear. All I could think of was that I was going to get in trouble for working an off-duty gig, but at the end of the day, I was a police officer, and I had taken police action. I could live with that.

I made my way back to my car and was relieved to see that my arm was uninjured. Luckily, no one got hurt. Well, except me. My pride was a little banged up, because despite my best efforts, one of the bad guys got away.

In retrospect, it might not have been the best decision to commandeer a horse and buggy, but every now and again I think about those people who were in the carriage that night and the story they will tell for years about the crazy New York City cop who gave them the thrill ride of their lives.

14

I Didn't Know That

MapQuest

We were in the Sixth Precinct doing a day tour, sitting in our RMP in uniform on Broadway at West Fourth Street. The West Village always managed to have a ton of people walking around all the time from all walks of life: working people, residents, shoppers, tourists, students, sightseers, you name it—and that day was no exception. I spotted a young guy walking down Waverly Place carrying a map case on his back. I watched him stop in front of a bicycle that was locked to a bike rack. He did a quick visual sweep of the area, but somehow didn't see us. He took the map case off, opened it, and pulled out a crowbar. He inserted the crowbar in between the bike's Chapman lock and the rack, applied a little bit of the pressure, and the Chapman lock snapped like a twig. I couldn't believe how effortless it seemed. We moved in and arrested him for larceny, but we didn't have a complainant. How could we know where the bicycle owner was or when they would return? But every time after that, whenever I'd see a messenger on foot carrying a map case, I'd ask him if he could help me out by letting me take a look at his map. Or if he knew where I could find a good crowbar.

The Daily News

We were on our way home from work after a day tour, sitting in traffic on Seventh Avenue South, waiting to get into the Holland Tunnel—a shortcut to Staten Island through New Jersey. We saw a young guy talking to a motorist while holding a rectangular box. They had a brief conversation, money was exchanged, and the motorist took possession of the box. We knew what this was all about, so we moved up to the guy, gestured for him to come over, and asked him what he had.

"VCRs," he said.

We asked him how much; I forget now what he was asking for them, but I asked him to let me see the box. It was wrapped very professionally in shrink-wrapped plastic, like it was fresh out of the appliance store, and he very confidently handed it over to me. I hefted its weight in my hands and then suddenly tossed it in the air. It landed about ten feet from our car with a thud. You might think that anyone else would have yelled out in protest that I was destroying his merchandise, but in that split second, he looked at us and we looked at him, and he knew immediately who we were. He might have even guessed ahead of time that we were cops, but greed got the better of him and he took a chance that we'd be gullible enough and be well into the tunnel with our purchase before we'd discover that we'd just bought a box of newspapers.

No Weapon Needed

One time we received a radio run of a "suspicious male". We rolled up on the scene and saw a guy loitering outside an outdoor café with a clipboard in-hand. He appeared to be soliciting funds from some of the café patrons for an identified charitable organization. We watched as he engaged them in brief conversation, jotted their names down on his clipboard, and collected money from them. The people had no idea why they were giving him the money; he asked, they gave. As it turned out, he was a complete phony. He was a polished, clean-cut grifter with a smooth line of bullshit. The only cause he was collecting for was his own. We locked him up and charged him with scheme to defraud—no weapon needed.

Check the Tires

Later on in my career, one of units I was assigned to was the Street Crime Unit (SCU). SCU turned out of Randall's Island, worked in plainclothes in unmarked police vehicles, and had the run of the city. One night, we were driving down Fifty-Seventh Street, and an RMP was directly behind us. We continued westbound when suddenly I spotted a young guy standing next to a parked car. I watched him make a handgun disappear under the left-rear wheel well of the car. Maybe he thought that the cops in the radio car behind us might frisk him, but it turned out the guy wasn't paranoid enough. He didn't make us (for cops), so we were able to grab him and we retrieved the gun from its hiding place where it was resting on top of the tire. I learned something that day; never limit the search to just the person. Check the surrounding area—even the tires.

Two Helmets Are Not Better than One

One night I was working a plainclothes off-duty gig in downtown Brooklyn. The gig was pretty boring—standing guard outside a medical office. I was looking around and noticed two guys standing next to a parked motorcycle. Each of them was holding a motorcycle helmet, so I thought they were getting ready to ride somewhere. Yet the longer I watched them, the more uncomfortable they became. And then it hit me—it wasn't their motorcycle. They were getting ready to steal it. *Damn, pretty slick*, I thought. But then they must have made me for a cop, because they ended up walking away, helmets and all. Yet another thing I learned by watching people and not taking anything for granted— sometimes things are not what they seem, or they are exactly what they seem.

Nobody's Home

One night while working in uniform in the Sixth Precinct, we responded to a call of a homeless man *squatting* (staying in a place illegally) inside a vacant room in a newly renovated building. It must have been a slow night because five other cops responded along with us. The door was unlocked, and we all walked in. There was a mattress on the floor, a lit candle next to it, and a paper plate of food next to that. Clearly someone had been there staying there recently, but it was just one room and no one was here now. Just as I turned to leave, I happened to see a shadow behind the door. Someone was hiding there. I announced, "Okay, guys, looks like nobody's here," while gesturing behind the door to the rest of the cops. I pushed the door against the guy, he yelled out, and we handcuffed him and charged him with trespassing. That was the first and last time I ever walked through a door without first looking through the crack of the jamb to see if someone was hiding behind it. If this guy had a gun, he could have easily shot all of us.

15

It Was a Snowy Day

Les and I were working a four-to-twelve in uniform, assigned to a sector car in the Sixth Precinct. We received a job (radio run) of a "10-20" (robbery-in-the-past). The dispatcher told us to see a male complainant at a residential apartment building in the east end of the precinct. We arrived at the scene and were surprised to find both the complainant and the perpetrator waiting for us. The victim told us that he had been approached by the male white who had attempted to tear his briefcase from his grasp. They struggled, and the complainant was able to get his bag back, but now the bad guy was sitting on the floor of the vestibule of the victim's building.

We approached the perp, who was slumped on the floor, and we figured out very quickly he was intoxicated. He looked like a construction worker; he was wearing construction boots and a *Carhartt* jacket. I don't remember what his side of the story was, but it was evident that he had, for whatever reason, tried to forcibly steal this guy's briefcase.

We stood him up, handcuffed him, and put him in the back of the RMP. Les stayed with him while I accompanied the complainant up to his apartment. We had to voucher (take back to the precinct) the briefcase as evidence, so the complainant asked if he could remove some papers that he needed for work and we agreed. I then wrote down the complainant's contact information for our reports and told him that the district attorney's office would be following up with him.

I took the elevator downstairs. As I exited the building, I could see Les standing outside the radio car. My first thought was, *Holy shit! Did he lose the prisoner?* But as I got closer, I saw that the prisoner was face down on the ground, and Les had his foot on his back.

Les yelled, "What the hell took you so long?"

Les was on a tear, telling me how the guy kept trying to escape, scrambling out of the car on one side, and then when Les would put him back in, he would try to get out on the other side. Les' frustration was rolling off him; this must have been going on the entire time I was in with the complainant. Finally, Les had stopped trying to put him back into the car and just stood on him until I came back down from the complainant's apartment.

Through no fault of ours the prisoner was now sprawled unconscious in the backseat, even though he certainly would have deserved it after everything he put Les through. We were halfway to the precinct, and the guy seemed to be down for the count. He was a big guy so I was already trying to figure out how we were going to get him out of the car, when suddenly he woke up, threw his construction-booted feet over the driver's seat headrest, and drilled Les

WHEN DID I START LOOKING LIKE A COP?

in the back of the head. Les' face was pinned against the windshield as he drove. I leaped over my seat to reach into the back to try to restrain the guy with Les yelling, "Get this asshole's boot off my head!" It came out kind of muffled, but I got the meaning.

Les jammed on the brakes and I attempted to wrestle the guy under control. We tried to get him out of the backseat, but he kept kicking us. It left me with no choice but to sit on him all the way back to the precinct.

Before we brought him into the station house, we "had a talk" with him, after which he became surprisingly docile and cooperative. Oh, and did I mention it was snowing?

16

THE ANGRY FELLOW

While assigned to the Sixth Precinct in NYC's West Village, I spent a few years assigned to the precinct's *Anti-Crime Unit*. Anti-Crime is an undercover detail within each precinct. The Anticrime Unit would generally work from 6:00 p.m. to 2:00 a.m. in plainclothes, patrolling the precinct in an unmarked vehicle. Sometimes the cops would even use their own private vehicles. If you found yourself without a partner because he or she was in court or on vacation, you had to work in uniform.

One day I was tour-changed to day-tour because my anti-crime team was in court. The desk officer assigned me to a foot post in uniform. I was on the corner of Sixth Avenue and Waverly Place when from behind me I could hear a male expressing his feelings about New York City cops. He was spewing the usual anti-cop rhetoric: Cops suck and they're always locking people up for bullshit.

"Fuck the police!" he yelled. "All cops are punk-ass motherfuckers."

He looked right at me and knew I heard him loud and clear. He ranted on for about twenty minutes more before storming off.

The next day, my partner and I were back out on the street in plainclothes. I spotted the guy from the day before. I told my partner what happened and suggested that we watch the guy for a while to see where he went. We tried following him with the car, but there was a lot of traffic, so I got out on foot to stay with him. After a few minutes, he decided to go into a supermarket on Sixth Avenue. I followed him in, and he went straight to the meat department. I watched as he stuffed about seven sirloin steaks into his jacket. He exited the store with me close behind. I radioed my partner to meet me on Sixth Avenue and West Eleventh Street. We stopped him there, identified ourselves as police officers, and questioned him as to his whereabouts for the last half hour. He claimed he'd just come from the subway and was walking uptown to meet a friend. I asked him if I looked familiar to him, and he said no. I asked him again, "Are you sure you never saw me before?"

Again, he said, "No."

I asked him to unzip his jacket, but he just looked at me until I asked to see what kind of steaks he had. He suddenly remembered who I was, and he knew the game was up. And while I certainly could have locked him up right there, I decided to give him a break instead.

"This is what's going to happen," I told him. "You're going to go back to that supermarket, ask for the manager, and tell him that you made a serious mistake. You stole some steaks, you're very sorry, and you want to return them."

He did as he was told, with me close behind, of course. Anyone else in my position might have sought revenge, but the store manager let him go on his way, and so did I.

17

Man With a Gun

One summer night, while I was still a rookie in the Sixth Precinct, my partner George and I were walking down Waverly Place on our way back to the station house. I happened to look to my right and saw a guy inside a black BMW, pointing a gun at this other guy's head. I turned to George and pointed across the street.

All he said was, "Holy shit ..."

We took up a position behind the car directly across from them, drew our service revolvers, and started yelling, "Police! Drop the fucking gun!"

When the interior light is on inside a car and its dark outside the car, you can't really see anything, so for a second they didn't know where the voices were coming from and seemed to be looking all around. Then the guy finally lowered his gun and we ran over, grabbed it from him, and pulled all three guys out of the car.

That was when one of the guys blurted out, "I'm a *C.O.*" (Department of Corrections Officer.)

We were like, *What the fuck is going on here?*

The C.O. seemed to think that because he'd told us he was a C.O., he should get his gun back and be able to leave. But we knew what we'd seen, and something wasn't right.

"Stand by, man," I said. "We have to call the boss (our sergeant) to the scene." We radioed for the supervisor and then brought the entire mess into the station house.

We may have been rookies, but it didn't take a first-grade detective to figure out what these guys had been up to, especially so close to Washington Square Park—a known location for drug sales. The real story was that these two corrections officers had come to Washington Square Park to try to score some free weed by shaking down a drug-dealer or two. They didn't figure on getting interrupted by two rookie cops who thought they'd stumbled upon a robbery-in-progress. The two corrupt C.O.s concocted some bullshit story to tell the sergeant, who was all too happy to buy it just so he wouldn't have to call in the duty captain.

The sergeant ended up shit-canning the whole thing, which we felt in our gut was so wrong. But it turns out that our instincts hadn't been: We thought we'd stumbled onto a robbery-in-progress, and that's exactly what it was.

18

I t was the dead of winter with nothing much happening, especially down on the west side of the precinct where it always felt twenty degrees colder as the wind blew inland from the Hudson. Les and I had Sector H-I on the four-to-twelve and decided to have our coffee down by the Pier.

It was a brutally cold night in February; snowing pretty hard with the wind whipping. Visibility was about ten feet in front of us. The area was desolate; no cars were parked, and no transactions were going down. We were closing in on the Salt Mines and I couldn't believe my eyes. There was someone walking toward us. As the figure got closer, I could see he was an elderly man wearing pajamas, a robe, and slippers. Covered head-to-toe in falling snow, he looked like the *Ebenezer Scrooge* character from *A Christmas Carol*. We jumped out of the car and approached him. He was barely able to speak and seemed unaware of the snow sticking to him and unaffected by the frigid temperature. I guessed he was heavily medicated.

He let us place him in the back of the radio car. While

we tried to find out what in the holy hell he was doing out in the middle of nowhere in his pajamas, I spotted a hospital wristband that identified him as belonging to Roosevelt Hospital.

Roosevelt Hospital? I thought. *That's way up in midtown Manhattan.* We radioed Central that we had a pickup of a disoriented person we would be transporting back to Roosevelt Hospital. On the way to the hospital we asked him some questions to try to find out how he got all the way downtown, but he couldn't remember. We were all lucky he was wearing the hospital bracelet. When we returned him, the hospital personnel knew immediately who he was, but no one told us how he'd gotten out or if they even knew he had gotten out. The man had no money and no identification. With conditions the way they were, he could not have survived. He would have surely died of exposure on that pier if we hadn't come along.

19

FLYING

O nce in a while, cops have to *fly*, which means be temporarily reassigned to another precinct that might be short of manpower for the tour. For this one particular four-to-twelve, I was reassigned from the Sixth Precinct to the Fifth Precinct. The Fifth covered Chinatown and I was assigned to a sector car with Jack, a Fifth Precinct cop who had even less time on the street than I had.

The Fifth was not one of my favorite places to work: It was crowded, the streets were narrow and filthy, and it always reeked of decaying garbage and other unidentifiable foul odors. Halfway through the tour, Jack and I received a job from the dispatcher of a possible *DOA* (dead-on-arrival). We responded to the location to investigate. We rolled up to the address—a decrepit, filthy, two-story walk-up. Our knock was answered by a middle-aged Asian man with a cigarette hanging from the side of his mouth. He stepped aside and gestured for us to enter. He apparently did not speak English, because he wasn't anything yet there was supposed to be a dead body at the location.

We glanced around the small apartment, but he appeared to be the only one there. We tried to communicate with him, but he did not even attempt to respond. Instead, he led us to what appeared to be the door to the bathroom. He pushed it open to reveal an elderly Asian woman hanging from the other side of it. I couldn't believe there was a dead body just hanging there, presumably his mother, and this guy was standing next to us displaying no emotion, with at least an inch of ash threatening to fall from his cigarette.

We were able to surmise that for some reason, the woman had committed suicide, but the son still said nothing. We made our notifications: *EMTs* (emergency medical technicians), the Fifth Precinct patrol supervisor, the Fifth Precinct Detective Squad, and the *ME* (medical examiner). Now all we had to do was wait. Then I realized I didn't have an identification tag (also known as a *95 tag* or *toe tag*), which we were supposed to affix to the deceased's big toe. I asked Jack if he minded going back to the Fifth Precinct to retrieve one, and he was all too happy to go.

I sat there with the son at the kitchen table, and neither us uttered a word. He was on his third cigarette, the ash still not flicked into an ashtray, no expression on his face. Suddenly he reached into his pocket, which of course had me reaching for my gun. He pulled out two twenty-dollar bills and gestured for me to take them. I removed my hand from my pistol. I shook my head and waved him off.

"No, sir. It's okay," I said.

He didn't understand a word but must have understood my body language, and returned the two bills to his wallet. There was a creaking sound and slowly the bathroom door swung open to reveal the old woman still hanging there. I was like, *What the fuck?* I looked at the son, and the ash finally fell from his cigarette. He just sat there, calm as could be, while his mother hung from the bathroom door, kind of looking at us.

Soon after that, EMTs and the patrol sergeant showed up, followed by the Fifth Precinct squad detectives and finally the ME. The scene eventually reverted back to standard DOA status while we waited for the morgue to pick up the body. When we finally got back out on patrol, I told Jack what had happened after he had left to get the toe tag. He shook his head and admitted he was glad he missed it.

After we went *EOT* (end-of-tour) back at the Fifth Precinct, we told some of the more seasoned Fifth Precinct cops what had happened. That's when one of the cops told us that sometimes older Asians living with their adult children feel they are too much of a burden and they end up taking their own lives to make their children's lives better.

20

THEY DON'T KNOW HIM

C ops normally work out of whatever precinct or command they are assigned to. But sometimes after making an arrest, the assistant district attorney (ADA) who had been assigned to write up the arrest would need more information than the arresting officer was able to provide at the time. The ADA would then send the arresting officer and his or her partner (even though they were technically not detectives) into the field to conduct an investigation and collect additional evidence and/or information. This was known as an *ADA's assignment*, and uniform cops didn't mind it, because it usually meant that they got to work in civilian clothes (out of uniform).

My partner Pete and I, who were regularly assigned to work out of the Sixth Precinct in the Village, received an ADA's assignment to locate the victim from an assault collar (stabbing) that I had made, but for some reason the ADA had us going to Brooklyn in uniform. At least we got to take a marked RMP.

On the way back from our assignment, I decided to

make a little detour to the longshoremen's hiring hall on Third Avenue and Sixtieth Street, the place where my father would go every morning to *shape* (see if he would be working that day). We pulled up in front of the hiring hall in the marked radio car. We got out and walked over to the front of the building where there were about five hundred longshoremen milling around outside. I walked up to one of the men and asked him where I could find Sal Belcastro. He told me that he didn't know him.

I walked over to a couple of other guys and asked them the same question: "Do you know Sal Belcastro?"

They each replied, "Nope. Don't know him."

I was getting a little annoyed, because I knew that everybody on the docks knew everybody else and could have easily directed me to where I could find my father, but even when I pointed to *Belcastro* on my nameplate and told them I was his son, they still insisted they didn't know the man I was asking about.

One of the guys must have finally gone inside to find Sal Belcastro and warn him that the cops were outside looking for him. They apparently never mentioned that I'd said I was his son. The ranks of the hiring hall closed in tighter around him.

It took some time, but eventually a message reached my father: *A police officer claiming to be his son was outside with another cop and wanted to see him.* A crew was dispatched to escort us inside.

Years later, when I saw the mob meeting scene in *Analyze This,* it reminded me of that day I had gone looking for my father at the hiring hall in Brooklyn. Longshoremen had an unwritten code down at the docks, too. If the cops ever come looking for a guy, remember: *They don't know him.* Even if the cop looking for the guy happens to be his own son.

21

PLainCLo†HES

A s I mentioned earlier, each precinct in New York City had an Anti-Crime Unit—an undercover unit within the precinct where the cops assigned wore regular street attire (plainclothes) instead of uniforms; they worked an odd tour, like 6:00 p.m. to 2:00 a.m.; and they patrolled the streets of the precinct in an unmarked car. What I didn't mention was the purpose of the Anti-Crime Unit, which was to target felony crimes occurring within the geographical area of precinct. Cops chosen for the precinct Anti-Crime Unit were cops who had already proven themselves in uniform to be hard-charging, street-smart cops who brought in high-quality arrests. There were roughly 200 to 250 cops assigned to an average precinct, with only six to eight slots in a precinct Anti-Crime Unit, so getting in wasn't easy. Staying in wasn't easy either; you had to be able to pull in at least two felony collars a month, every month, or risk losing your spot.

While I was assigned to the Sixth Precinct, my partner and I patrolled in uniform, but that didn't get in the way of us busting our asses to make all kinds of collars. I was already averaging two felonies a month or more in uniform, so when the day finally arrived that I was chosen for Anti-Crime, I was as ready as I would ever be.

For the longest time I had believed that the only thing getting in the way of me making some really great arrests was that I was in uniform and the bad guys could see me a mile away. I had figured that now that I was in plainclothes, making felony arrests would be so much easier, like shooting fish in a barrel. It wasn't long before I realized that it wasn't as easy to make those felonies as I had thought it would be. It may have been our job to find the bad guys, but it was the bad guys' job to know who and where we were, or else they couldn't do their job, which was robbing and burglarizing and the like. Making two felony arrests a month was going to be tougher than I had imagined.

The Sixth Precinct had experienced a recent spike of robberies and larcenies on West Fourteenth Street. Even though I wasn't wearing a uniform, the perps had no trouble making me as a cop. I quickly realized that if I was going to be effective, I'd have to get creative. Knowing I would have to change up my appearance, I came into work one day wearing a crazy-looking hat with huge pom-poms hanging off it. I had a pair of eyeglasses with Scotch tape on the nose piece, a raggedy old coat, and a bag of cans. The guys on my team thought I was nuts—just the look I was going for.

I was *deep*—which meant I could walk around, talk to myself, and look through the garbage, and no one gave me a second look. It was like I was invisible. I walked up and down West Fourteenth Street keeping a close eye on things, when suddenly I heard a commotion across the street near Fifth Avenue. I quickly turned around and saw that some guy had ripped a chain from another guy's neck. The thief was charging right toward me, so I ducked behind the newsstand. As he passed, I jumped out, tackled him to the ground, pulled my gun out, and yelled, "Police!" He was terrified, right up until he realized that I actually was a cop, at which point, believe it or not, he let out a sigh of relief.

I radioed the Anti-Crime Team to meet me at my location; they interviewed the victim, and we locked up the perp. But it just goes to show you that the bad guy would apparently rather face a cop, even if it meant being arrested, than some psycho. Dressing up like a lunatic, no one wants anything to do with you, including the bad guys.

22

Piano Keys

O ne winter day my partner Les and I were working a four-to-twelve tour on West Fourteenth Street in the Village in plainclothes. I had grabbed an old coat and wrapped a huge scarf around my head and face, so only my eyes were visible. I got out on foot and started walking around to see if I could identify any potential pickpockets. I kept in touch with Les just in case I started following someone. It was brutally cold out, so it was kind of slow that day with not a whole lot going on.

The key to successfully following people is to walk in the opposite direction of them; keep crossing the street, and try to stay in the crowd as much as possible. You have to stay deep; keep a loose tail and never lose sight of them. Avoid making eye contact, or the person might get raised-up and walk off.

A couple of hours into the tour I spotted a guy changing direction several times; he kept walking up and down the block and crossing the street. I radioed Les a description of the guy. We followed him for about three hours with him having no idea we were there. It seemed like he just couldn't find the right person to pickpocket. The streets were starting to get thin. Just when we thought that he was giving up, he spotted a guy and girl walking arm-in-arm. I watched him tuck in behind this couple and begin to move in closer and closer. I noticed the girl's handbag was patent leather and had a huge piano-key design on the side of it. When the pick was directly behind them, I saw him reach into the girl's pocketbook and start to remove her wallet. I was directly across the street and watched the whole thing go down, but I did not have enough time to notify Les of what was happening before some woman walking in the opposite direction of the couple turned around and yelled out to them, "Hey, he's trying to steal your wallet!"

Lady, would you shut the hell up? I wanted to yell. But it was too late.

I ran across the street, calling Les on the radio. The pick saw me, realized I wasn't selling trinkets, and—*boom*—he took off. We didn't have to chase him too far before we caught him and cuffed him, with me wrenching my thumb in the process. Once in the precinct, he admitted that he had noticed me walking around, but the head scarf made him think I was just one of the regular Fourteenth Street vendors.

I will never forget that pocketbook with the piano-key design, as I am sure neither will the pickpocket. He's also not likely to forget the day he got locked up by a guy in the head scarf. Twenty-nine years later whenever it is cold out, I am left with yet another reminder of that arrest: my aching thumb.

23

BOX CUTTER ROBBER

E ven though each precinct had their own Anti-Crime Unit that was tasked with targeting felony crimes within the confines of that precinct, each Patrol Borough Command within the NYPD had a Robbery Squad. There were eight Patrol Borough Commands in total, and they were geographically designated: Manhattan South, Manhattan North, Brooklyn South, Brooklyn North, Queens South, Queens North, the Bronx, and Staten Island. Each Patrol Borough Command was further broken down into divisions; each division was numbered and consisted roughly of three precincts.

The Robbery Squad in each borough was a central repository for the identification and enhancement of robberies that seemed to happen more than once and had similar characteristics and, therefore, fit a pattern within that borough. Once a robbery pattern was established through some common denominator—either similar descriptions of the same suspect, the same weapon used in each robbery, or recurring similarities in execution—the Robbery Squad would compile the information and issue a bulletin that would be communicated to all the precincts within the Patrol Borough of occurrence.

We had been in the Sixth Precinct Anti-Crime Unit for a while now, making our quota of felony arrests and then some. On occasion information would come down from the Manhattan Robbery Squad (MRS) about a robbery pattern that the precinct Anti-Crime Units should be aware of. The latest robbery pattern was happening in the confines of the Twentieth Division, which consisted of the Sixth, Tenth, and Thirteenth precincts.

The pattern was a robbery with a weapon, and the weapon being used was an orange box cutter. There had been at least fifteen robberies fitting this pattern, committed by one individual, and one of the victims who had been robbed was a woman in the vestibule of her building holding her baby. That really got us motivated to catch the guy. But when we reviewed the complaint reports of the people who had been robbed, there were many inconsistencies in the description of the suspect. Accounts of his height, weight, clothing description, and race all differed from victim to victim. I knew from experience that this could happen, especially when you had many different people victimized by the same perp—the descriptions will vary. But one thing they all remembered the same was that he had a ponytail and was armed with an orange box cutter.

When our Anti-Crime team turned out that night, it wasn't long before I spotted a male Hispanic who partially matched the description of the robbery-pattern guy we were looking for. I saw the ponytail and remembered that it as part of a victim's description. We pulled over and I jumped out, switching my radio to point-to-point so I could talk to my crime team without interfering with the Central Dispatcher. I followed him as he frequently changed direction, following people who were alone and carrying groceries, and I knew in my gut this was our guy.

With the help of the team, we managed to follow the suspect for four hours without being made. At one point he flagged down a Sixth Precinct radio car and I thought that was it; the uniform cops would recognize him as the box cutter robber, and all our work would be for nothing. But they thought he was a regular guy on the street; after a few words were exchanged, the RMP rolled on.

The guy took his time walking up and down the streets looking for the right victim, but I guess something didn't feel right to him that night, so he finally gave up and headed for the subway at Sixth Avenue and West Fourth Street. I couldn't let him get away; I felt it in my gut that it was him. So we followed him down the subway stairs to the train, grabbing him in front of the token booth. A quick *toss* (search) and what did we recover from his jacket pocket? You got it—the orange box cutter.

Back at the Sixth Precinct, we saw the two uniformed cops who had briefly spoken to the box cutter robber on the street, and we asked them what he had said to them. They told us he flagged them down to tell them about a possible injured male on Christopher and Hudson streets. Maybe he was trying to send them on a wild-goose chase to get them out of his way.

We transported the box cutter robber to the Manhattan Robbery Squad. They placed him in a lineup where he was positively identified by several of the victims he had robbed.

It was a great feeling to know that the guy responsible for fifteen or more open felony cases had been apprehended by us. Sometimes what may seem like an insignificant detail that people remember about a crime can be the one thing that helps it get solved. We paid attention to the details, and another dangerous guy was taken off the streets.

24

I'M a GiRL

Ozzie and I were working plainclothes in the Cabaret District of Greenwich Village, the east side of the precinct not far from NYU and Washington Square Park. There were plenty of bars, open-air cafés, and street musicians; it was the middle of summer, and the streets were packed. This was prime pickpocket season, so we kept our eyes peeled for picks working the area. We had to stay sharp, because there was a lot going on.

With all the street vendors selling their wares, it was the perfect crowd for a pick. We walked up and down the streets trying to spot someone changing direction or getting in close behind people. Suddenly I spotted a small male black following a young couple very closely. I got Ozzie's attention and we started tailing him. It wasn't long before he got in close behind a young girl carrying a small black handbag slung over her left shoulder. I watched him as he moved in directly behind her, reached over, unsnapped her bag, removed a bottle of water first and then her wallet, *put the water back*—and *boom*—done, smooth as silk. The victim didn't feel a thing. I had to admire his skill.

We grabbed him and took him over to the back of a van, and suddenly he yelled, "I'm a girl! I'm a girl!" The *he* was a *she*. It didn't mattered to me whether she was male or female, she was still *going* (getting arrested) for grand larceny and criminal possession of stolen property (CPSP).

We brought her into the precinct, got her pedigree information, had a female officer search her, and then brought her back into the precinct's cell area. While my partner ran her name in the database to search for prior arrests, I started fingerprinting her but quickly saw that she was practically fingerprinting herself. She was very polite and cooperative, and I could not help but admire the way she had performed out in the street. She was definitely no stranger to the arrest process.

A few minutes later my partner came back with her rap sheet—a rap sheet that told us she had forty-two prior arrests, mostly for drugs and grand larceny. She admitted to me she had a crack habit, which is where all the proceeds from her pickpocketing went. She was this tiny person; she would be lucky to weigh in at eighty-five pounds, and I found myself feeling bad for her.

The time had come to transport her to Central Booking, and it would be the last time I would ever see her. People might think, *Who gives a shit about this person? She was a crackhead and a pickpocket.* But she was still a person—a person who had gotten caught up in the crack epidemic and was struggling to find a way to survive. I had to hand it to her; she was good at what she did, but I couldn't help but think if only her circumstances had been different what she might have been able to accomplish in life. *Crack addict*, *pickpocket*, but underneath it all, yes, she was still *a girl*.

25

THEY GOT ME GOOD

We arrived at Manhattan Central Booking (MCB) late one Saturday night with a couple of arrests. The cells were packed; it was standing-room only. We couldn't even lodge our prisoners in the holding pens because they too were filled to capacity. We waited outside for word that we could bring our prisoners back in. But I had to use the head (bathroom), so again I knocked on the "nasty brown door", as we called it. The door had a tiny square of a window with what appeared to be all kinds of fluids stuck to it. Like always, it took a few minutes for someone to open it, but they finally let me in. Just inside the door of MCB there was a small podium where you would normally wait with your prisoner until they were ready to take his Central Booking photo. There were two cops standing there, flanking their prisoner.

I started to move past them when the prisoner looked right at me and said, "What the fuck are *you* looking at?"

I thought, *What the fuck?* But I said, "You better shut that filthy sewer of yours, shit-for-brains!"

He yelled back in my face, "If I didn't have these cuffs on, I'd kick your bitch-ass all over the place!"

I thought he had to be out of his fucking mind to speak to me like that, and I was more than a little pissed off that the officers guarding him weren't doing anything about it.

"Who in holy hell do you think you're talking to?" I yelled back, my blood boiling.

The cops finally told him to shut up, but he ignored them and kept on running his mouth. I demanded that the cops take "those fucking cuffs off." With that, their prisoner immediately removed his hands from behind his back and said, "Oh, yeah, motherfucker?!" and started laughing his ass off. Instantly it hit me and all the cops started laughing; even some of the prisoners joined in—because the prisoner wasn't a prisoner. He was a cop.

26

THE OLD HANDKERCHIEF SWITCH

Working the streets day in and day out, you begin to recognize certain interactions between people and whether those transactions are business or casual in nature. We would observe people's movements, the type of clothing they were wearing, if they were constantly changing direction, or if they stopped people on the street and engaged them in conversation. Whenever the conversation began to get lengthy, we knew we might possibly have a scam in progress.

One day Les and I observed a male black stop a young female Hispanic and start up a conversation with her. He showed her a small piece of paper, and they started walking together. Immediately we knew what we had. We watched them enter a Burger King on Sixth Avenue and West Fourteenth Street. They both sat down at a table, and I followed them in my best homeless-man disguise: raggedy jacket, eyeglasses with a Band-Aid in the middle, furry hat with pom-poms hanging down, and, of course, a bag of cans. I talked to myself loudly while keeping an eye on the guy and the young girl. I could hear him telling her he had a confirmed winning lotto ticket but that he was in the United States illegally and afraid to cash it in out of fear of being deported.

This was all bullshit, but these unsuspecting, gullible people fell for it every time because the story was plausible and the guy seemed very believable. The guy told her that all he needed her to do was cash in the ticket for him and that for her trouble she would receive half of his winnings. By the expression on her face I knew she believed him, and seemed excited by the prospect of sharing in the windfall.

Here's how the guy gets over: He explains that in order to trust her, he needs something valuable of hers to hold on to (cash, jewelry, a watch) and they will arrange to meet up later to do the exchange. At that time, her valuables would be returned for his share of the lottery winnings. He suggested she turn over her watch and jewelry as a show of good faith; after all, she had the confirmed winning ticket, right? I watched as the girl took off her earrings and watch and he handed her the lottery ticket. He wrapped the earrings and watch in a handkerchief and stuffed them into his pants pocket. Another player instantly appeared on the scene and confronted the guy.

"That's not how you hide shit," the other man told him. The second man told the first guy to give him the wrapped-up jewelry. He pulled out a different handkerchief, rewrapped the jewelry, and stuffed it down inside the front of *his* pants. "That's the way it's done," he said, then removed the handkerchief from his pants and returned it to the first guy. The first guy appeared grateful for the advice.

The first guy told the girl to meet him at a certain

location at a given time, except now the second guy, who has left the scene, is actually the one in possession of the girl's jewelry and watch. The first guy has a handkerchief full of tissues down the front of his pants. The girl is left with a worthless, bogus, forged lottery ticket; no jewelry; and the promise of a meeting that will, of course, never take place.

Luckily for the girl, I had watched the whole thing go down. Just as the two guys tried to make their escape in a cab, Les and I pounced on them and locked them up. We managed to get the girl and bring her back to the scene, where we explained the whole scam to her. She broke down in tears. We really couldn't blame her for wanting to believe that she could become rich so easily. This is the way of the street: people prey on innocent people who just want to believe that it could be their lucky day. And as it turned out for this girl, it was.

27

TIME TO GO

I t had been 1988 when I got into the Sixth Precinct's Anti-Crime Unit. During the four years that followed, my partners and I had made hundreds of collars: *car boosters* (breaking into cars), grand larcenies, burglaries, robberies, drug sales, and assaults. The Sixth was a great place to work: the friends, the laughter, and even the tears. But I felt somehow that I had gone as far I could there. I yearned to get out into the heavier commands, where "shots fired" was commonplace, taxi-livery robberies were a daily occurrence, and car stops turned into vehicle pursuits. It might sound crazy to some people, but this is how motivated I was. I wanted to be hitting a different high-crime precinct each night, on the big stage, out on the street, observing, following, pursuing, and making arrests for serious felonies on a larger scale.

I had put in for a transfer to the citywide Street Crime Unit, and it had finally come through. I was on deck. I was going in the game.

28

THE STREET CRIME UNIT

I had been in the Anti-Crime Unit in the Sixth Precinct for four years, but a precinct Anticrime Unit, even though you were undercover, had its limitations. You had to stay within the geographical confines of your precinct unless you were in hot pursuit for a violent felony. I wanted—hell, I *needed*—to experience what it was like to work in some of the highest-crime areas of the city, and for that, I had to be in Street Crime.

On January 10, 1992, I was transferred to the Street Crime Unit. I had finally made it to the most elite plainclothes unit in the New York City Police Department. The unit consisted of approximately eighty cops handpicked from every precinct in the city. These guys weren't just cops. They were the best of the best; they had keen instincts and quick reflexes. They could recognize suspicious activity when others might be oblivious.

Street Crime had citywide jurisdiction; they got to work in every high-crime precinct in the city. Commanding officers of precincts would request Street Crime come into their command to work because they were getting hit hard with robberies at gunpoint, homicides, and other violent crimes. Each night when they turned out, the Street Crime squads would go to different commands in each borough to work, because the precincts were inundated with violent crime. Brooklyn, Queens, Manhattan, and the Bronx—they could go anywhere in the city.

The Street Crime Base was located on Randall's Island under the Triborough Bridge. It was in an old NYC Parks Department building that had been taken over by the NYPD. I was assigned to C-Squad; the tours were 2130 to 0600 hours. I arrived at Street Crime Base early that night and parked in front of the command. It looked nothing like a precinct; NYC Parks Department logos were still on the front and throughout the inside of the building. There was even a screen door on the main entrance—not the exactly the fortress I had envisioned.

I walked in and was confronted by thousands of photos of guns taped to the windows of the small offices where civilian administrators worked. I couldn't believe how many gun collars these cops had; I was both impressed and intimidated.

The lockers were downstairs, so I went down and grabbed the best I could salvage out of the shittiest lot of lockers I had ever seen in my career. I cleaned it out as best I could, hoping not to find remnants of past crimes forgotten. When I was done, I took a walk around the base. It felt strange to be there; it wasn't like a regular precinct. I hoped to measure up to these warriors who came from all over the city, each one with an outstanding reputation from wherever they'd come from. This was a pivotal point in my career—a decision I would never come to regret.

29

I'M ON THE SHEET

My first tour in Street Crime was on a cold January night. I got partnered up with a cop nicknamed *Turtle* (real name *Jimmy*). Turtle was a really cool guy from upstate New York. We hit it off pretty good right out of the gate. We turned out of Randall's Island doing a 2130-by-0600 tour and ironically got assigned to work in the Sixth Precinct in the West Village, the precinct I transferred in from. I had just left there a few days ago.

It seemed like my old command was getting hit pretty hard with strong-arm robberies in and around the Cabaret Area on the east side of the precinct. Little cafés and restaurants with live music and open-air seating covered most of Bleecker Street from Sixth Avenue to LaGuardia Place.

We no sooner got within the confines of the Sixth when we picked up a radio transmission from an officer on a foot post. He was reporting that a female had just been robbed by two male blacks. They took her cash and fled in an unknown direction, and the victim didn't know if they had weapons. We headed in the vicinity of the robbery location to see if we could observe anyone running or engaging in any type of suspicious activity. When we got to the corner of West Houston Street and Sixth Avenue, I observed two male blacks exchanging clothing and turning some of their stuff inside-out. We followed them to Carmine Street and Sixth Avenue. We didn't have much else to go on at that point; there was no real description such as height, weight, color of clothing, direction of flight, or, most importantly, if they had weapons. All we knew was what we had seen: two guys frantically changing clothes on a frigid night out on a city street, but that was enough to have me thinking these guys could be the robbers.

We approached them, identified ourselves as police officers, and asked them a few questions like, "Where are you guys coming from?" and "Why are you changing clothing?" We also asked for basic pedigree-type information (name, address, etc.). None of their answers made any sense, so we tossed (searched) them for weapons and radioed the officer on the foot post who had originally put the robbery over the air. We informed him that we had two *possibles* (suspects) and gave him our location.

A few minutes later a radio car pulled up to the scene with the complainant (the woman who was robbed) in the backseat. I walked over to the car and asked the lady if she recognized the two guys, and she emphatically stated, "That's them! They stole my money!"

This method of identifying suspects at the scene is known as a *show-up*, where the victim is given the opportunity to make a positive identification shortly after the crime has been committed.

We searched the guys again and recovered the stolen money and a few other items that they had taken from her. We had had very little to go on, but by keeping our eyes open and our instincts sharp, we caught the right guys, and they were *going* (getting arrested). My very first night in Street Crime, and I was "on the sheet"—made my first arrest in SCU— and I had my old command, the Sixth Precinct, to thank for it.

30

THE COLOR OF THE SHIELD

I had been in Street Crime for a few months, working in different precincts all over the city. It was exciting to work in commands that before I had only seen displayed on the collar brass of cops I worked with at details and funerals. Street Crime worked at night, when most of the city's crimes occurred. There was a sign that hung in our base that read "We Own the Night." It bore a caricature of *Muggable Mary*, a little old lady walking with a cane, representing the famous undercover female police officer who worked in the unit and was one of the original decoy cops to work the streets.

One night when we were doing a four-to-twelve (evening tour), we got a "10-02" (report back to the Street Crime Base). On the way back I wondered if I could have possibly done anything wrong, and in a few minutes I was about to find out. We pulled onto the island (Randall's), and I reported to my *C.O.* (this time "C.O." means *Commanding Officer*).

"Sit down, Joe," he said with a serious look on his face.

Uh-oh, I thought. I sat.

He started to explain that he'd received a call from a lieutenant in Special Frauds, an investigative unit that dealt exclusively with criminals committing confidence game, fraudulent credit card, and pickpocket schemes.

"Joe, they want you to come in for an interview," the captain said.

"Sir, I just got here. Besides, I never even put in for that unit ..."

"I know, Joe, but they must have been looking at your past arrest record, which included a host of pickpocket and confidence game arrests, and they are looking for you to come on board."

My C.O. was a great guy, a real cop's cop, and he knew that more than anything, I had wanted to stay in Street Crime, but he advised me to go down to Police Headquarters to speak to the lieutenant in charge of the unit and listen to what he had to say. Reluctantly, I agreed.

"So when do they want me down there?" I asked.

"Right now," he said.

"*Now*? Sir, I do not have any business attire or anything in my locker—"

"Don't worry about it. They already know that."

I grabbed one of SCU vehicles and headed over to *1 PP* (Police Plaza). All the way there I thought to myself, *How the hell did this happen*? I didn't have any hooks (people in high places within the NYPD who could pull strings to get you where you wanted to go), and I had never even heard of the Special Frauds Unit until that day. I arrived at headquarters and asked some cops working there if they knew what floor Special Frauds was on. They'd never heard of it either. They looked it up for me, and I took the elevator to the tenth floor. I followed signs for *Special Frauds*.

I found the office filled with rows of desks and guys in suits on phones. I was a street cop through and through, and I found the sight of these cops sitting at desks with guns strapped to their waists unsettling. Except for some awards and police pictures and statues, it looked an insurance office. Before I became a cop, I would never have imagined that real cops would ever be working in an office environment. I guess it was just the cop in me thinking that all cops should be out in the street locking people up (except for detective squads, of course). But then I realized that these little-known units hidden within Police Headquarters played an integral role in the operation and management of the world's largest police department.

I located the lieutenant (who turned out to be a total gentleman), and he began to explain why he'd brought me down, as well as two plainclothes transit cops who were not present at the time. It would seem that as a unit, Special Frauds was not making many arrests. In fact, the lieutenant informed me that they'd only made ten arrests for the whole year. He seemed a little embarrassed. So in an effort to improve their productivity, they began to review the arrest records of cops who had made more than a few of these types of collars (confidence games, pickpocket, etc.), and they came up with the two transit cops and me— pretty impressive if you think about it. I knew I had a lot of experience making those types of collars and that's why I had been called down.

The lieutenant went on to tell me that he wanted to assemble a team to go out and make bona fide confidence game and pickpocket arrests—do what we did best, follow people engaging in that type of criminal activity and bring in some good numbers.

Wow, this is really cool, I thought. *I get to be out there, doing what I love to do, following people, observing them committing these acts, and then locking them up.* Sounded easy, right? But it really wasn't. You really had to be sharp and possess the ability to observe certain behaviors in those individuals, stay with them for hours, hope you didn't get made, and, on top of all of that, actually see the crime go down. I knew I was up to the task, because I'd already proven it over and over.

I finally allowed myself to get pretty excited about the prospect of being part of an elite team that would be targeting fraud collars throughout the city and possibly getting a gold (detective) shield out of it. Over the weeks to follow, I went for two more interviews with Special Frauds. Then, finally, the lieutenant called me and gave me the news that the police commissioner was adamant about not putting a "white shield" (regular cop) in the unit; he wanted someone who was already a detective (gold shield).

My biggest disappointment was the fact that someone could think that the color of a shield determined ability, ability to make the kinds of arrests that could only be made by cops like me, cops who knew exactly what to look for and got results, no matter what color my shield was.

31

YOU NEVER KNOW WHOM
YOU MIGHT BE DEALING WITH

We were doing a four-to-twelve tour, getting ready to turn out of Street Crime Base, headed to the Forty-Seventh Precinct in the heart of the Bronx. Wayne, my regular partner, had to do a day tour because of a court appearance, so they assigned me a new kid—a kid I'd heard only got to Street Crime because his father was a chief. Already I wasn't happy. To make matters worse, the captain (Executive Office of Street Crime or, as we referred to him, the "X.O.") decided he wanted to ride along with us this particular night. I was officially in hell.

The X.O. was a strange character; he looked like Mel Brooks and wore goofy-looking ties. He was always telling jokes that weren't funny, and he didn't know the streets. None of us knew where he'd come from, how he'd gotten to Street Crime, or why he even wanted to be there. What we did know was that he needed to stay at the base and out of everybody's way. There was a reason and purpose for

Street Crime, and that was to get the guns off the streets and lock people up for violent crimes. It was no place for an inexperienced cop, no matter what the rank. And the kid they saddled me with was no better. He was so green, he couldn't find a bad guy in Central Booking. Between the two of them, I was in for very bad night. A headache started to bloom.

My headache and I geared up, grabbed a set of keys, and set out to find the car in the lot. I headed over to the drivers' side of the vehicle like I always do, when the captain said he wanted the kid to drive. I couldn't believe it; I *always* drove—it was the unwritten agreement between me and my partner Wayne. I was seething as I took my place in the backseat of the car and we made our way over to the Four-Seven Precinct. To make matters worse, I had no choice but to listen to the captain's ridiculous jokes and keep an eye on the kid who didn't know where he was going or what he should be looking out for. I felt like a prisoner myself.

We were cruising the vicinity of White Plains Road when I spotted a vehicle driving erratically up and down the side streets. The captain was, of course, in the midst of telling another one of his stupid jokes when I blurted out, "Pull these assholes over!"

The kid was oblivious and said, "What?"

So I repeated my directive. "Pull these guys over!"

SCU cars were not equipped with sirens, so he threw the portable flashing red light on the dashboard and got in behind the vehicle, which suddenly stopped in the middle of the block. I never took my eyes off the guys as I exited our vehicle, but the kid and the captain were, of course, looking somewhere else and totally missed the guys taking off. I yelled, and we jumped back in our vehicle and gave chase. I got on the radio to tell Central what we had; I put over a description, and we were in pursuit. We didn't know who these guys were; whether they were armed, or even if they were *wanted* (had a warrant). All we knew was that they were running, and they must have been running for a reason.

This kid couldn't drive for shit. It was like being trapped in the backseat of one of those little cars at the amusement park where you never seem to get anywhere. Thank God the Four-Seven Precinct cops were on the ball. Within a few minutes, they had spotted the car and gave chase. They managed to apprehend one of the occupants who had ditched a handgun in a backyard as he ran, but they were able to recover the gun the next day.

The Four-Seven cops called us to respond to the scene where they had grabbed the guy. As a general rule, when a police unit puts over (transmits on the radio) a pursuit or information about a crime occurring in the past and the perps are apprehended by another unit (a different team of cops), it's their arrest unless that unit doesn't want it, and the Four-Seven cops didn't want it. So we handcuffed the guy and brought him into the Four-Seven Precinct for processing. We charged him with Reckless Endangerment. We couldn't charge him with the gun, because the cops didn't see him in possession of it.

A few days later we learned that the guy we apprehended was a suspect in five homicides. And while there had been several witnesses to the murders, the witnesses had been terrified to testify, because they feared retaliation. A few months later we were told that the same suspect was wanted on some heavy federal charges. He was finally tried and convicted, receiving a minimum of fifty years in federal prison.

This goes to show that what may have appeared to the inexperienced eye like a simple case of driving recklessly, a sharp street cop knows differently. People thinking they can do the job just because they landed in the unit without bringing with them the requisite skills and experience, are not just endangering themselves, but the cops working alongside them. It's a matter of life and death.

'KILLING MACHINE' GETS 50 YEARS

By PHILIP MESSING

A Bronx man cops call a "killing machine" suspected in more than half a dozen murders was sentenced yesterday to a minimum of 50 years in prison for slaying two brothers.

Calvin Buari, 24, received consecutive terms of 25 years to life from State Supreme Court Justice Joseph Cerbone for the 1992 slayings of Elihah Harris, 31, and Sal Haddin Harris, 26.

Buari was convicted Oct. 31 of killing the brothers in their car at 213th Street and Bronxwood Avenue in the Gun Hill section after one of the victims made a remark that insulted Buari, according to testimony.

Cerbone said Buari demonstrated a "callous disregard for human life" whose "presence in the community has caused untold grief and tragedy for the family of the deceased."

Buari is awaiting trial on another 1993 murder, and sources said a gun they believe is linked to Buari was used in two other killings.

32

SOMETHING JUST DIDN'T LAY RIGHT

O ne night, my partner Tommy and I turned out of
SCU and were assigned to the Four-Six Precinct in
the Bronx. Keeping our eyes and ears open as usual,
we spotted a livery cab on Webster Avenue. Cabbies were
constantly being robbed, so the NYPD came up with a
program to help them. If a cab driver affixed the program
sticker to the back window of his cab, then the police could
pull him over at any time to check on him and make sure
he was okay.

We spotted the sticker on this cab's rear window, threw
our red light up on the dashboard, and honked our horn
to signal for the livery cab to pull over. We could see one
male black passenger in the backseat. We pulled in behind
the cab, keeping a safe distance where we could observe
every movement inside the vehicle. When we got up to the
car, Tommy approached the driver's side and explained to
the driver why we had pulled him over. I positioned myself

on the rear passenger side, blading my body in a strategic tactical position where I could see what the passenger was doing, but he would have to turn all the way around to see me. Tommy had finished explaining to the driver about the program (of which he was already aware) and whispered to me over the roof of the cab, "The passenger's left jacket pocket seems really heavy."

I moved forward a bit, bent down, and politely asked the gentleman, "Do you have a gun?"

To which he replied, "Yes."

I looked back at Tommy to gesture that we had a positive response. I then asked the passenger to step out of the vehicle. Tommy came around to my side. We frisked the passenger and recovered a .22-caliber, eight-shot pistol from the passenger's left jacket pocket without incident or injury. Every gun collar should go that smoothly.

It takes a sharp street cop to recognize something that ordinarily might be overlooked by an untrained observer— something like a pocket not laying right or weighing heavier than normal, especially in the winter with all the extra layers of clothing that people wear when it's cold out, but Tommy spotted it. He was right, and we're still here.

Thanks, Tommy.

33

THIS TIME IT'S "ONE STRIKE, AND THEY'RE IN"

My partner Tommy and I turned out of Street Crime Base driving an old, beat-up Mercury the size of the *USS Intrepid* aircraft carrier. It was a piece of shit—an old NYC taxicab without the taxi light on top but the same yellow color. We were working a day tour in the confines of the Four-Two, one of the worst precincts in the Bronx. All the precincts in the Bronx were pretty bad, but when you drove around the Four-Two—with its nasty buildings; empty, dirty lots; garbage all over the place, and packs of wild dogs roaming the streets—it was like a throwback to the sixties. In this piece of shit car, we fit right in.

We cruised the area, looking for any type of suspicious or criminal activity. We pulled up to a stop sign, glanced to our right, and observed a dark-colored Toyota with the engine running and the windows down. As we passed it, we saw a red gasoline rag wrapped around the rear license plate, like a signal of some kind. No one who knew that neighborhood would ever leave their car with the engine running and the windows down—and I mean no one, not unless they never wanted to see it again. Tommy and I figured this vehicle was probably stolen, and pretty soon someone was going to come along, jump in, and take off. So we drove around to the other side of a huge abandoned lot, got into position where we could observe the car, and waited.

About ten minutes went by before we saw a male Hispanic jogging up the block toward the vehicle we were watching. When he got a little closer to the car, I saw that he had what looked like a dark-red stick in his hand. Once he was next to the car, he rubbed the stick against another smaller stick. It ignited, and he threw it into the Toyota.

Tommy and I looked at each other and said, "Holy shit! It's a flare. He's torching the car!"

As soon as the flare hit the backseat, a car came screaming up the block, the guy jumped in, and they took off. We scrambled around the lot and got in right behind them. There were three other males in the vehicle. We radioed Central to get a Four-Two Precinct car to back us up. Central asked for our location and a description of the vehicle. We switched our radios to the Four-Two Precinct division and told them what we had. In a split second, a Four-Two radio car was there. I put the red light on up on the dash and watched as the guys in the car all turned around at the same time like, *What the fuck?* They couldn't believe we were right on them.

We pulled them over, placed them all under arrest, and took them into the precinct for arrest processing. We recovered a full box of flares in their backseat. They were both disappointed and perplexed; they could not understand how they'd gotten caught. We learned afterward that they had torched another vehicle on the same block. We charged them with arson and criminal possession of an incendiary device.

Looking back on it, these guys were pretty slick using a flare instead of just throwing gasoline inside the car. It had made sense; a flare is slow-burning, wouldn't draw attention to them, and would give them time to make their escape. Except that they didn't count on Street Crime to pick on their act and put it out as faster than they could get it started. One strike, and they were in (custody, that is).

34

R olling out of Street Crime Base on yet another cold winter night in New York City, Wayne and I were doing a 2130-by-0605 tour of duty, headed for the confines of the Midtown North Precinct. Midtown North covered Hell's Kitchen, one of New York City's more infamous neighborhoods. Hell's Kitchen, home to the *Westies* (a gang made up of Irish immigrants whose main trade was extortion and burglary), had been cleaned up for the most part as lower-income residents were pushed out. But during this time in the mid-nineties, it was seeing its share of people getting their vehicles stolen or broken into. Thieves would gain access to the car by breaking the small rear vent window. Spotting a broken vent window was usually a reliable indication that the car, or its contents, had been stolen.

We were coming up the west side of the North when we spotted a vehicle occupied by three male whites with the small, rear vent window broken. We started following them, while I scoped out a good location for a car stop down on Eleventh Avenue in the fifties. I threw the red light up on the dashboard and beeped the horn, indicating for them to pull over. As soon as we had them stopped, we had to immediately jump out of our car, because we saw that the passenger in the right front seat had gotten out. As the operator (driver) of our car, I was the one to approach the driver's side of the vehicle, so I kept an eye on the driver and the passenger in the seat directly behind him. Wayne addressed the guy who'd jumped out of the car on the passenger side.

"I'm 'on the job'," he said too quickly as Wayne made his approach. "I work in the North. Why are you bothering us?"

"On the job" was common terminology among cops. It was typically the first way an off-duty cop would identify him-or herself to an on-duty cop if he or she happened to get pulled over, which happened often enough. But something about the guy's mannerisms had our instincts telling us otherwise. A *real* off-duty cop, no matter how inexperienced, knew not to jump out of the car like that on a car stop. Something about him just wasn't right.

Wayne and I looked at each other, not sure what to believe. Wayne noticed the guy's jacket hanging heavier on one side, so he reached out to feel the jacket pocket. As he grabbed the guy's jacket, he felt what he was sure was a *speedloader* (an apparatus that holds bullets to enable faster reload of a revolver) in his pocket.

"The guy's got a speedloader!" Wayne yelled to me.

The guy then attempted to shove Wayne backward over a snowbank leftover from a previous storm. Wayne struggled for balance as I left the driver's side of the car and tackled the guy to the ground. I handcuffed him, and Wayne ordered the other two occupants out of the car and put them to the ground as well.

As I searched the self-proclaimed cop, I yelled to his buddies, "Is this asshole a cop?"

They both shook their heads. I found a loaded revolver in his jacket pocket—silver, clearly not a cop's weapon.

We handcuffed the other two guys and requested another Street Crime Unit to "85" us at the scene. Our S.C. lieutenant responded as well. We were standing outside with the cop impersonator when the lieutenant came walking up and asked us what we had. I had started to explain when suddenly "the cop" spit in the lieutenant's face. We now realized the time had come to speak to this guy in a firm manner and explain that this kind of behavior was completely unacceptable and would not be tolerated. We kept on explaining this to him all the way to the precinct, yet we remained unconvinced that he had gotten the message.

We arrived at Midtown North, brought the three guys into the station house, and began processing their arrests. While Wayne was filling out the paperwork, I went outside to inventory their vehicle and voucher it as evidence. As I was searched the car, I recovered another handgun and a bag full of what we cops refer to as "burglar's tools" (screwdrivers, hammers, pry bars, etc.) and. This told us that our guy was more "Wannabe Westie" than make-believe cop, as these were the tools of a Westie's trade. The cop imitator would be going to jail not only for criminal impersonation of a police officer, but for two counts of criminal possession of a weapon. His two passengers would be going for possession of the gun found in the car.

Some cops might have been intimidated when pulling over someone who identified himself as a cop. There's a tendency to want to be "cool" and just wave them on, but our instincts told us otherwise, and our instincts turned out to be right. It was a good arrest. Not only did no one get hurt, but it turns out that the cop impersonator had violated his parole, which meant that after his hearing, he was going back to prison for a long, long time. He had better hope his fellow inmates didn't find out he was "on the job."

35

WHat ARE tHE ODDS?

One night, my partner Timmy and I turned out of the Street Crime Base driving a yellow cab. We were cruising up Sixth Avenue in the confines of the Midtown North Precinct when we observed the driver of a *real* yellow cab falling asleep while he was driving. We saw he had one male passenger in the backseat, so we followed him for a while. We decided to pull him over to see if he was okay. It must have looked funny, a yellow cab pulling over another yellow cab, but I'm guessing the flashing red light on our dashboard gave away our police status.

I approached the vehicle on the driver's side and asked the driver if he was all right. I looked at the male white passenger in the backseat and saw that he was shaking. I gestured to my partner for him to open the door on the curb side so he could get a better look at the passenger. I then asked him the same question I asked the taxicab driver, "Are you okay? Why are you shaking?"

He didn't respond at first, so I asked, "You don't have a gun on you, do you?"

He responded, "Yes."

Out of all the New York City taxicabs roaming the streets of the city on any given night, we happened to stop the one cab with a guy in the backseat who has a gun on him and *readily admitted to it.* While this was not the first time someone I had stopped gave me an honest answer, the odds of it happening were still pretty incredible.

We brought him into the precinct for arrest processing. When we ran a name check on him for prior arrests and/or warrants, we found out he had a prior arrest for armed robbery.

Some people might find this story hard to believe, but this is the kind of thing that happens when you're out on the street and you remain curious and vigilant. You can never know what a situation might develop into. You have to be able to determine which behaviors raise a red flag, and how to ask the right questions. And every now and then, you get the right answer.

36

Bad Credit Score

My partner Bernie and I were doing a day tour in the confines of the Nineteenth Precinct. We were heading northbound on Madison Avenue around Forty-Eighth Street when I spotted a middle-aged male black looking through the glass window of a high-end electronics store. Ordinarily, no big deal, but there was something about him (besides his yellow pants and flowered shirt) that caught my attention.

I told Bernie that I wanted to get out on foot and watch the guy for a while. He dropped me off, and we maintained radio communication with each other. I took up a position across the street from where I first observed him. From across the street, I was able to watch him through the reflection in the store window. He paced up and down the block, went back to the original electronics store, looked in the window, and walked away again. Something was up, but I didn't quite know what it was yet.

About twenty minutes passed by when the guy walked off once again and headed to the corner. This was all happening in the days before beepers and cell phones. The next thing I saw was a female white emerge from the electronics store. She hailed a cab as a store employee carted out all kinds of electronic equipment and helped her load it into the trunk of the cab. I hadn't radioed Bernie yet because I still didn't know if I had anything. I watched as the woman got into the cab, the cabbie drove to the same corner where the male black was standing, and the man joined her in the cab. Then they took off.

I got on the radio and told Bernie, "Pick me up. I'll fill you in when you get here."

Bernie came screeching up. I hopped in, and we struggled to keep up with the cab. I told Bernie what I'd seen, and he didn't ask me any questions, even though I knew he was as curious as I was as to what was going on.

After going through several red lights trying to keep up with the maniac cab driver, we finally caught them and pulled the cab over. I exited our car, kept an eye on the passengers, and noticed a lot of shoulder movement in the back seat. That raised me up to the possibility that they were trying to hide weapons or drugs. I ran up to the right-rear passenger side of the cab. Looking through the window, I saw both passengers throw stuff to the floor by their feet. I flung open the door as the last item hit the floor and immediately saw that it was a credit card. I looked further inside and saw several credit cards and drivers' licenses next to their feet, and that was when I realized what was going on. They were ditching these items because they were stolen. When I asked them if the items on the floor belong to them, they adamantly denied it.

We told them to step out of the cab and handcuffed

them. We collected the identification cards and credit cards from the floor of the cab and brought everything into the Nineteenth Precinct. During booking, they continued to play innocent, insisting, "I don't know what you're talking about," trying to convince us that everything we recovered from the floor of the cab was already there when they got in it. They had tried to sell that story all the way into the precinct, but we weren't buying it.

Once in front of the Nineteenth Precinct desk officer, we were able to conduct a more thorough search and found a few more credit cards that they had stuffed in their socks. Using some of the information from the identification cards, we were able to track down the owners. One of the items was an ID card from an employee who worked at the Waldorf Astoria Hotel. *Bing*—it all started falling into place.

What we had were two pickpockets who *hit* (pickpocketed from) three different people in the Waldorf Astoria hotel. They then took the stolen credit cards and employee identification, went straight to a high-end electronics store, and charged about $2,500 worth of electronics on the stolen cards. One victim I spoke with hadn't even realized that her credit card was missing. That's how quickly these grifters work.

37

MaMa's Got a Gun

My partner Tommy and I were cruising down Webster Avenue in the confines of the Five-Two Precinct when we observed a small vehicle in front of us speed up and then slam on the brakes. It did this several times for what seemed to be no legitimate reason. We got up close behind the vehicle and observed that there were three occupants, a male driver and two female passengers. We continued to follow them for a couple of blocks, and he kept swerving the vehicle from lane to lane. We had finally seen enough. We pulled him over.

He realized who we were immediately and stopped his car abruptly in the middle of the street. We got out of our car and approached the vehicle with our guns drawn—Tommy on the driver's side, me on the passenger side. Suddenly the right-rear door flew open, and a pistol fell out into the street. I yelled to Tommy that we had a gun on the ground. The passenger in the seat closest to where the gun fell out was an older female Hispanic who blurted out that the gun belonged to her.

We ordered everyone out of the vehicle and handcuffed them. Through preliminary questioning, we were able to determine that the driver was the son of the older woman, and the younger female was his girlfriend. We never got to the bottom of why the kid was driving like an asshole. My gut was telling me it was his gun, but we had Central run his name at the scene, and it came back clean (no warrants). The mother maintained the gun was hers. We asked her why she had a gun, and she said it was for protection against her ex-husband. There was nothing more we could do; the mother insisted it was her gun, and it was recovered in her immediate vicinity. We had our gun collar, no one got hurt, and it looked like baby boy was going to let his mama go to jail for him.

We had had no choice but to release the two kids at the scene and bring the mother into the Five-Two Precinct for arrest processing. When we finished, we put her in the car and headed down to Bronx Central Booking (BCB) when suddenly the woman started complaining. She said she was on medication for anxiety attacks and now she wanted to kill herself.

"I'm not going to make it through the night," she warned us.

Yet before we had left the precinct, she seemed fine. This was more than likely a stall tactic; people often think that if they say that they need to go to the hospital, somehow they won't have to go to jail. All it really does is prolong the inevitable, but we didn't have a choice; once she said she was sick, we had to bring her to a hospital to get her checked out.

One of the difficulties when having to get medical treatment for prisoners is that you can't just take them to the nearest hospital. Only certain hospitals were approved to treat prisoners, and even fewer were approved to treat *female* prisoners. The only hospital authorized to evaluate female prisoners at that time was Woodhull Hospital in the confines of the Eight-One Precinct in Brooklyn. And so the adventure began.

We notified our Street Crime supervisor of the situation and made our way to Brooklyn. Throughout the transport, Mama's "condition" seemed to be worsening; she had begun screaming and howling for no apparent reason. We finally arrived at the hospital and they were (of course) swamped; knee-deep in other *EDPs* (emotionally disturbed persons) all waiting their turn to be evaluated by the attending psychiatrist. We waited hours for her to been seen—so long that we were about ready to see the doctor ourselves. It was a total clusterfuck. After a while, we didn't even care about the overtime anymore. We just wanted to get the fuck out of there and lodge the nut bag in BCB.

At last, it was Mama's turn. She was examined and released back to us. We left Woodhull and shot back over to the Bronx, submitted the paperwork to the Central Booking sergeant, and were finally rid of her. We made sure we ran out of there before she could start screaming and howling again, but maybe she learned a valuable lesson not to take the rap for her son. We sure learned one: just when we thought we had a "ground ball" (easy collar), things could just as quickly turn to shit. The one good thing to come out of it was that we got another gun off the street.

38

AMBULANCE CHASERS

It was a hot summer night at about 0200 hours, and we were in the confines of the Seven-Seven Precinct in Brooklyn. My partner Wayne and the SCU sergeant were "lights out" (asleep) in the car. Even though I was as tired as they were, I forced myself to remain alert for fear of someone being able to get the drop on us, in which case then we'd never wake up again.

We were parked next to a housing project, so I knew instinctively there were many eyes on us. Plainclothes, unmarked car—it didn't matter; we were far from invisible. They knew we were the police, and believe me, they hated our guts. We couldn't see them as they watched us from the shadows, but we knew they were there. This was the type of location where reports of "shots fired" were a regular and very real occurrence.

Seemingly quiet nights like this one always held the potential for a homicide or robbery. I had been out on the street for a long time now, night after night, making car stops, questioning people, investigating suspicious activity, being as proactive and motivated as I could possibly be. If experience had taught me anything, it was that anything and everything could happen at any given moment. I kept an eye out for that anything (or anybody) that would warrant investigating.

Suddenly a light-blue vehicle raced past us, jammed on the brakes, then reversed at a high rate of speed. The driver appeared to be frantically searching for someone. He made a quick U-turn, came back again, and then sped off.

I yelled at my guys, "Wake the fuck up. I think we have something!" They immediately snapped to and asked me what was up. I pulled in tight behind the blue car and followed him to Atlantic Avenue near Saint Mary's Hospital. He slammed on the brakes again and jumped out of his car. He had spotted what he was looking for: a male black with a backpack, which turned out to be *his* backpack, taken from his vehicle moments earlier, a situation his upstairs neighbor had alerted him to as it was occurring. The driver of the vehicle then pulled out a handgun and started chasing the guy.

All of us could see what was happening now, so we jumped out of our car to chase the guy with the gun who was chasing the guy with the backpack. The foot pursuit had us weaving in and out of parked ambulances. We finally grabbed the guy who had the gun and the guy who had the backpack, but both were empty-handed; neither one had anything. Clothes from the backpack were strewn all over the street, but we didn't see the gun. We searched all over, retraced our steps, and looked under ambulances, but there was *no gun*. We really hadn't been all that far from the gunman during the entire pursuit, so it wasn't making sense that we weren't able to recover the gun.

I was pretty frustrated and was just about ready to abandon the search when I saw what I thought was a ball of the guy's folded-up socks that I came across lying in the street. I nudged it with my foot and—*zang*—there was the gun stuffed inside them. I could not get over how randomly kicking at that ball of socks uncovered the weapon we had been searching so hard for. We were like little kids rejoicing in our find.

When the neighbor told the guy that the other guy (who didn't have the backpack yet) was breaking into his car, the guy ran back into his apartment, grabbed his gun, and hopped into his car to chase him down. When he'd caught up with the thief, he pointed the gun at him, and the thief panicked and threw the backpack back at him. In turn, the guy with the gun realized that at some point the police had joined in and that it would not turn out well for him if he was caught with an illegal handgun. Somehow, amid all the chasing and dodging in-between ambulances, he had managed to stash the gun in the balled-up socks. I had been pretty impressed with the speed in which the guy had been able to hide the gun, especially with all the running around we were all doing. If we had not been able to recover the gun, we wouldn't have been able to charge him with the possession of it.

Both of the guys were getting locked up; the "victim" for menacing and illegal gun possession and the thief for larceny (of the backpack) and criminal mischief (damage to the car). We brought both of them into the Seven-Seven Precinct for processing. We finished all the paperwork and headed down to Brooklyn Central Booking. We lodged our prisoners and then I reported to the District Attorney's (D.A.'s) office to have the criminal complaint drawn up by one of the ADAs (Assistant District Attorneys).

It was a well-known fact that the Brooklyn D.A.'s Office *hated* Street Crime. Street Crime held the record for making the most gun collars of any unit within the NYPD, but the Brooklyn D.A. apparently did not believe Street Crime could possibly make so many gun collars *legitimately* and so they were forever scrutinizing our methods. They were notorious for "D.P.ing" (declining prosecution of) our arrests, which meant that they didn't believe the stories behind how we came to make the arrests in the first place, but seriously, could I have made this shit up?

39

One and Not Done

Rolling out of Street Crime, my partner Wayne and I were assigned to the Three-O (thirtieth) Precinct. It had been a pretty slow night, despite the fact that the Three-O was one of the busiest *houses* (precincts) in New York City. The humidity hung in there even as dawn signaled the end of yet another hot and sticky summer night. It was 0540 hours; we had twenty minutes left to go before end of tour. The streets were empty except for a few people making their way home from whatever club they had gone to and even fewer people on their way to work. Despite the heat, the windows of our car were always down, because we wanted to be able to hear what might be going on, like calls for help or shots fired.

We were headed north on Amsterdam Avenue at 153rd Street when—*crack*—we heard a shot go off. It sounded like it came from somewhere nearby, so we slowed down to look all around the immediate area. I looked to my right and saw a couple pushing a baby stroller; kind of unusual for that time of morning. I looked at them and they looked at us. Wordlessly, I communicated my question with an imperceptible nod of my head in their direction: *Do you know who fired that shot?* The male pushing the stroller answered with an ever-so-subtle nod of his own. *Yes,* and he gestured in the direction of the two male blacks who had just passed them. *It was those two assholes. Can you believe they're firing a gun out here in the street while I'm pushing my baby in a stroller?*

Okay, so I didn't really get *all* of that from him, but I still thought that what had passed between us was pretty cool.

We swung the car around and headed in the direction of the two male blacks. There was no question they made us, so we jumped out of the car. We identified ourselves as cops. One of the guys stopped immediately, but the other kept on walking as quickly as he could until he was around the corner and out of sight. Wayne grabbed the one guy, while I took off after the guy who kept going.

As I caught up to him, I heard the sound of metal scraping across concrete. He must have tried to slide the gun away from him. I handcuffed him quickly, retrieved the weapon from across the street, and brought him back to where Wayne was holding the other guy. We ended up releasing Wayne's guy, because we reasonably believed I had the guy who had actually fired the shot.

We headed into the Three-O Precinct to process the arrest. When we finished with all the paperwork, we left to transport our prisoner down to Manhattan Central Booking (MCB) for lodging. Proper tactics is for one cop (usually the arresting officer) to sit in the back with the prisoner during transport. I was driving, so Wayne sat in the backseat and the prisoner sat to the right of him. We were traveling southbound on Seventh Avenue somewhere around West Twentieth Street when we spotted two male Hispanics stealing what looked to be two bags of US mail that had been left next to a mailbox. I hit the brakes, and Wayne jumped out on foot and gave chase. It all happened so fast. I knew it was not the best tactical move I could have made, but I had to help my partner. I chased the mail thieves, cutting them off with the car and holding them there until Wayne could catch up and handcuff them. All the while I kept an eye on our original prisoner in the back seat.

We now had three collars, but we had to bring the two new perps into the Three-O Precinct for processing before we could continue on to MCB with our first prisoner. We brought all the prisoners in front of the desk officer who eyed us suspiciously. As we were from the Street Crime Unit, he couldn't have a clue as to who we were or what we had, so of course the first thing he asked was, "Who the hell are you guys? And what is this shit you're bringing me?" (Translation: *What unit are you from, and what did you arrest these individuals for?*)

We identified ourselves as being from Street Crime, and he just shook his head. He knew Street Crime had citywide jurisdiction and could make arrests in any precinct within New York City at any time and in any place. The Street Crime Unit was to the NYPD what the U.S. Marine Corps was to our country's military forces: "Any clime, any place."

Once we explained to the desk sergeant what we had and how we had it, we quickly got busy processing the two additional arrests. But while I was filling out the paperwork, Wayne came up to me and told me that the two assholes we caught stealing the mail were offering him a bribe to let them go. After a quick discussion, Wayne and I decided to go with it.

We approached the desk officer again, who couldn't be bothered to hide his annoyance with us for infiltrating his precinct in the first place. Knowing it wasn't going to improve his opinion of us any, we told him what had just happened. It was bribery, and he had no choice but to notify the Field Internal Affairs Unit (FIAU). FIAU was a unit within the NYPD's Internal Affairs Bureau whose work in the field was primarily focused on finding cops doing something wrong, but their other purpose was to assist those very same cops whenever someone tried to bribe a cop. Our feelings about having to call them for assistance were mixed, but protocol mandated that they had to be notified to respond to the precinct to document the bribery offer and to help capture the bribery electronically.

Back when I was in the Police Academy, I was led to believe that the New York City Police Department, the largest police department in the world, was also the most sophisticated when it came to high-tech, state-of-the-art surveillance equipment. So I guess after waiting hours for FIAU to show up, I was more than a little disappointed that the tape recorder they wanted us to use to record the bribery offer was as big and bulky as a thick paperback novel. How was Wayne supposed to conceal it on his person? What happened to high-tech? The only thing missing was a flashing red light and a prerecorded message saying, "At the sound of the beep, please repeat your bribery offer again now." Wayne was never going to be able to pull it off. We complained, but it fell on deaf ears.

"This is what they give us," FIAU said.

Wayne stuck the recorder inside his hooded sweatshirt, trying to conceal it as best he could. He went back into the cell area to see if he could get the guys to mention the bribe again. But they were having none of it. The fact that FIAU had taken so long to get to the precinct in the first place, coupled with the obvious bulk of our "hidden" recording device, must have spooked them.

Sure enough, within a few minutes, Wayne reemerged from the holding cells with a disappointed look on his face. Wayne had gone in there, trying to get them to repeat the bribery offer and hoping they didn't notice the bulky recorder in his sweatshirt. He asked the prisoner how much money he was talking about giving us to let them go, but the guy wouldn't answer. He clammed up and never said another word. He kept staring at Wayne's pen—*Wayne's fucking pen*—because he must have thought it was a microphone. He never even noticed the bulky tape recorder in Wayne's sweatshirt; he was focused only on the pen. Well, at least someone thought the NYPD was high-tech.

40

On another Street Crime tour in the Bronx, Wayne and I had just turned the corner onto Webster Avenue from Marion when we spotted two male Hispanics coming down the rear fire escape of a building. We pulled over to observe their descent. When they hit the ground, they climbed a huge fence, and that was when we confronted them.

"What's up, bro?" I asked. No response. "Police," I said. "What's going on? Do you guys live in that building?"

But they weren't answering, so we separated them and questioned them again. They were playing that *No-habla-ingles* bullshit, but Wayne and I had picked up enough street Spanish to fake our way into making them believe we spoke the language. One guy's story was that they'd gotten locked out of their place and had tried to get in through a window; the other guy said they were visiting a friend. We knew it was all lies. So we brought them back into the building and asked them to show us what floor they lived on. It was obvious to us they just chose some random floor, but we went with it. For our own safety, we had already searched them for weapons, so we all piled in the elevator and pushed the button for the fifth floor.

When we got off the elevator, they pointed to an apartment that they clearly did not have access to, so we told them to sit down on the floor while Wayne and I tried to figure out what these assholes had really been doing in the building. We were sure they didn't live there and hadn't been legitimately visiting anyone. Yet all we had at this point was trespassing (a violation), which was a bullshit charge, especially when there weren't any "no trespassing" signs in front of the building. Theoretically, anyone could walk in.

The two assholes were still trying to bullshit us when I heard a door behind us creak open. A young female Hispanic peeked through the narrow opening. She gestured for me to come over to the door. Wayne kept an eye on the two guys, while I went over to speak with her. She was trying to explain in her best broken English that she had been in the elevator with the two guys. The guys had sexually assaulted her, grabbing her breasts and buttocks. She was terrified and embarrassed and couldn't stop crying. I tried to console her and at the same time convince her that she needed to come forward if we were going to be able to do anything about it. But she just couldn't bring herself to give us any more information, refusing even to give us her name. Maybe she wanted us to know what they had done to her in the hopes that we could take care of it without her actually having to be involved, but the law doesn't work that way. Without her cooperation or other witnesses or injuries, without any cameras in the elevators, we couldn't arrest them. They would get off scot-free. She closed the door on us, and that was that.

Wayne had grown up in the Bronx and was a great street cop, a real stand-up guy. I walked over to him and explained what had happened. We discussed the situation for a few minutes and decided that what the situation called for was a "re-education session". We were pretty confident that by the time the session was over, those guys would think twice before ever doing that to a poor defenseless girl again, especially in that building.

41

END OF THE LINE

We were doing a 2130-by-0605 tour, working in the confines of the Four-Six Precinct. It was a pretty quiet night as far as jobs went (911 calls). Suddenly the radio started crackling with the voices of a Four-Six Precinct unit: "Shots fired! Davidson Avenue! 85-forthwith!" (police officer needing help immediately). We were nearby, so we got to the location in a heartbeat. Wayne and I pulled up just as four uniform cops were hurrying from the building. When we identified ourselves as Street Crime, they asked us to secure the crime scene while they transported the cops involved in the shooting to the hospital for trauma.

We acknowledged their request and ran into the building from where the shots had been fired, not really knowing what we would find. Apparently the uniform cops had chased a male Hispanic into the building. The suspect managed to get through the first entrance door, but the second door was locked. Knowing he was trapped, he turned and aimed his weapon at the officers in pursuit. The officers opened fire, shooting him in the head.

When we entered the vestibule, we saw the male Hispanic lying on the steps. His eyes were wide open, his breathing was labored, and there was a bullet fragment on the step where it must have exited his head. Sirens in the near distance told of the bus' (ambulance's) impending arrival.

I took one look at him and told Wayne, "This guy is done."

Wayne and I stood over him, knowing that our faces were the last ones he was ever going to see in his miserable existence. Wayne uttered a couple of words in the form of "last rites"—not what you would call your standard eulogy, but something that a cop might say for someone who had just tried to kill another cop. It was too late; he couldn't hear us. We stood over him and watched as he drew his last breath. It was the end of the line for him.

42

TIME'S UP

I was working with Tommy and Jeff on a rainy, windy night in the South Bronx. It was Jeff's first night back on patrol since his line-of-duty injury several months earlier. We were cruising down the Grand Concourse near 149th Street in the confines of the Four-Four Precinct when we decided to pull over a livery cab for a routine safety check. It looked like the cabbie had one male black passenger in the back of his cab. I threw the red light up on the dashboard and beeped the horn, signaling for the cabbie to pull over. He readily complied, and we proceeded to conduct our safety check.

I approached the driver, identified myself as a police officer, and asked to see his driver's license, while Jeff and Tommy came up along the right-rear passenger side of the cab. I glanced in the backseat and saw that the passenger was wearing a neon-orange hunting outfit, the kind a hunter might wear in the woods so he wouldn't get shot by other hunters. There wasn't exactly anyplace to go hunting in the Bronx, but this was the style at the time.

I examined the cabbie's license and was in the middle of asking him if everything was all right when suddenly a gust of wind blew his license right out of my hand and sent it floating down the Grand Concourse. At the same time, Jeff yelled, "This guy has a gun!" and yanked the passenger out of the backseat.

Both Jeff and Tommy restrained the guy, handcuffed him, and recovered the handgun. All of this went down pretty quickly. We had the perp in custody, and no one was injured. We were good to go. I had decided to try to locate the cabbie's license when Jeff blurted out, "Hey, Joe, do you know who this is?"

I came around to the other side of the cab and looked at the guy closely. I took in the neon-orange jumpsuit and the huge clock hanging from his neck. The thing had to be ten inches across, no joke; it was bizarre. I looked from him to Jeff and said, "No, Jeff, I have no fucking idea who he is."

"Flavor Flav!" Jeff announced proudly.

Who the hell is Flavor Flav? I thought as I shook my head at Jeff's reaction. Jeff told me Flavor Flav was a famous hip-hop artist, which explained why I had no idea who he was, but it didn't explain how Jeff *did* know. I might have been the *last* guy to know rap or hip-hop artists, but I had thought Jeff would be the *second to last* guy. As Jeff talked about him, I seemed to recall seeing a little black guy on TV wearing a diaper, an Uncle Sam hat, and a big clock around his neck. It was the *same clock,* now that I thought about it, and this must be the *same guy*—the one and only Flavor Flav. I guess I should have been happy he wasn't wearing the diaper.

We headed into the Four-Four Precinct with Flavor Flav

in handcuffs. Tommy was "up" (it was his turn to make an arrest), so he was taking the collar. Post-search, Flav was also found to be in possession of a few jumbo vials of crack. Flav was very upset that his fans might find out about the crack, so he pleaded with us to *shit-can* it (make it disappear). The gun was apparently okay with Flav; getting locked up for possession of a weapon would actually boost his street cred. But getting caught with drugs would only tarnish it.

"No dice," I told Flav. "That's not how it works. You're going for both."

It may sound Boy Scout-ish, but I never forgot what we were taught in the Academy: "Honesty and integrity are the cornerstones of good policing."

Flavor Flav—he wasn't such a bad guy. I guess his time was just up.

FLAVOR FLAV
Was on probation.

Rapper Flav busted in Bx. on gun, crack raps

By PHILIP MESSING

Flavor Flav, who's had more arrests than hit records in recent years, was busted in The Bronx last night on charges of illegal possession of crack and a loaded gun.

The 36-year-old rapper, whose real name is William Drayton, was arrested at 9:30 p.m. when cops from the Taxi and Limousine Task Force pulled over the livery cab he was riding in on the Grand Concourse near 156th Street in the Melrose section.

Officers Thomas Sommerville, Joseph Delcastro and Jeffrey Salta, who were making spot checks, ordered Drayton, who was the only passenger, to get out.

When he did, he began to reach into his waistband, but was stopped by one of the officers, who seized a loaded .380 caliber Davis automatic from him, police said.

The weapon contained five rounds, police said.

A later search turned up three vials of crack cocaine that Drayton was carrying, police said.

Drayton, who was wearing the trademark large clock that he hangs down his chest, was dressed in an orange hunting outfit and had little to say after he was taken into custody.

The rapper, who performs with the group "Public

43

OUT-OF-State Pursuit

My partner Wayne and I were doing an overnight, riding along the service road of the Cross Bronx Expressway, when we observed a small gray Toyota without headlights speed through a stop sign. The vehicle was being operated by a male black, and he had a female black passenger in the front seat next to him. We pulled in behind them, threw the red light up on the roof, and started beeping the horn, but they refused to pull over. They picked up speed and disregarded every traffic signal in their path. We were officially in pursuit. We radioed to notify our supervisor and gave him our location, which of course was rapidly changing as the chase continued.

The Toyota suddenly jumped onto the Cross Bronx, headed for the George Washington Bridge. We thought we might have a kidnapping on our hands, because we could see the female flailing her arms and screaming at the driver. We maintained communication with the boss and other Street Crime Units and updated them on the direction of flight and whether or not we could see if they had any weapons. The Toyota was an older model, not well maintained, and the driver didn't handle it well, especially at a hundred miles per hour. He swerved in and out of lanes as he neared the George Washington. We radioed the boss that we were approaching the lower-level entrance to the bridge and would soon be crossing state lines into New Jersey. We were gaining on him, and for one brief moment I had pulled alongside him. There we were, side-by-side, and he dared to make eye contact with me.

"I'm going to fucking kill you!" I mouthed while waving my pistol at him.

The fear on his face told me he knew I meant business. He punched the accelerator and pulled ahead of us again, pushing his car to the limit.

We were over the bridge and headed onto Route 80 when the driver suddenly lost control of the Toyota and hit a ditch dividing the Interstate. The small car catapulted into the air and flipped over onto its roof. All I could think was, *Oh, God, I hope they're not dead.*

We jumped out of our vehicle and approached the overturned car cautiously, looking around for weapons as we pulled open the passenger doors. We pulled the female out; she was shaken up but otherwise fine. We then went around to the driver's side to drag the asshole driver out, and surprisingly, he too seemed to be uninjured. A few pointed questions later, he admitted that he ran because he had an outstanding warrant and didn't want to go to back to jail.

"That's *it?*" I said, stunned. I couldn't believe it. I was beyond disappointed that we had gone through all that for nothing. It was what we in Street Crime referred to as a "no hot lunch" (or no-gun) situation. There we were—we risked our lives, driving like psychos, thinking we might have something really good, because *who in their right mind would run like that if they didn't have something really bad to hide?* Yet, it turned out to be bullshit.

When the New Jersey State Police rolled up on the scene, they explained their "absconding law" to us, which meant they would be taking the arrest off our hands. We escorted them back to the trooper barracks and gave them our information. Then we headed back to our state and our base, glad to be done with it.

44

My partner Jeff and I were patrolling within the confines of the Four-Four Precinct near Yankee Stadium when I observed what appeared to be a twelve-year-old boy driving a vehicle just coming off the Major Deegan Expressway. We pulled in behind the car and noticed that it had three occupants. The driver looked so small I could barely see his head above the door sill when I pulled alongside. We thought the car might be stolen, so we signaled for them to pull over.

I approached the driver's side, while Jeff came up on the passenger side of the vehicle. Jeff got there a few seconds before me and warned me that the occupants had blood on their clothing. We took a few steps back and drew our weapons, ordering the occupants to exit the car slowly, hands up where we could see them. As the two in the front got out, I noticed one guy in the back was shifting from side to side. We cuffed the first two and put them to ground, but the guy in the rear seat still hadn't gotten out of the car. We knew that meant he was attempting to hide something.

We'd had enough of his stall tactics. I showed my impatience by yelling at him, "Get the fuck out, now!"

He finally did, and we handcuffed him. Jeff watched the suspects, while I did a thorough search of the backseat. Knowing that some of these vehicles have removable backseats, I gave it a tug and it lifted up easily. A fully loaded .38-caliber revolver had been hidden underneath. I shouted "Mohaska!" to Jeff (this was our code word for *gun*, adopted from the movie *The Untouchables*) to let him know what I'd found. We then transported all three of them to the Four-Four Precinct for arrest processing. Their blood-soaked clothing remained a mystery; even after all the citywide inquiries to see if there might be a connection to a serious assault or homicide, we still came up empty.

It took a few months before I received a notification to appear in Bronx Supreme Court for a *suppression hearing* (on the admissibility of evidence) regarding the arrest. All three defendants were present, each one with his own legal-aid attorney. One of the attorneys asked me where I recovered the gun from. I replied that I had found it under the rear passenger seat of the vehicle where the defendant had been sitting.

Suddenly the judge yelled at me, "Where exactly *was* that?"

I started to respond by saying, "Your honor—" but she cut me off.

"Don't '*your honor*' me!" she snapped.

What was this woman's problem? I thought I had been pretty clear in the way I had explained how the backseat was removable, but she refused to listen. She tore off a sheet of paper from the pad in front of her, thrust it at me with a pen, and ordered me to draw her a "diagram" that would illustrate what I was describing. *Was she kidding me? I couldn't draw.* And I would have guessed that even the best artist might have some difficulty drawing the backseat of a car. Sadly, I realized that if the outcome of this case depended on my artistic ability, it was already lost. But there I was, doing my best to sketch something that even remotely resembled the rear seat of the Toyota, even going so far as to draw an arrow pointing to where I had found the gun.

I handed the judge my rendering, and she was not amused. In fact, she looked at it with disgust. She didn't see it, and I knew at that moment that she never would. There would be no further questions. The judge was anti-cop and not afraid to show it. She had suspended logic; her mind was already made up and the outcome of the hearing was a foregone conclusion before I even took the stand. I could have been Rembrandt, but the only thing she could *see*—the only conclusion she would draw—would be her own: cops routinely planted evidence and framed innocent people. Case closed.

45

PUSHED tHE WRONG BuTTon

My partner Jeff and I were doing a day tour, driving around the vicinity of White Plains Road within the confines of the Four-Seven Precinct. The Four-Seven was a hotbed for drug sales and possession of illegal guns. We observed a vehicle speed through two stop signs with its headlights off. We followed the male Hispanic driver for a couple of blocks before throwing the red light on the dash to let him know we were stopping him. He complied by pulling over to the curb.

We exited our vehicle, approaching slowly and cautiously. I came up on the driver's side of the car and opened my usual round of questioning with, "How you doing, buddy? What's going on? Do you know that you just sped through a stop sign, and you don't have your headlights on?"

His mumbled reply was something to the effect of, "Oh, I didn't even see the sign."

And I was thinking, *Really? No shit.* I asked him for his "paperwork" (driver's license, registration, and insurance card). He began to rummage around the interior of his vehicle as if the documents I asked for *should be there* somewhere. I watched him carefully while he rooted through the glove compartment, when all of a sudden I caught the upward movement of the trunk lid out of the corner of my eye. He was either purposely trying to distract us or he must have accidentally hit the trunk-release button, but we would find out soon enough. With a nod to Jeff for him to keep an eye on the driver, I went to the rear of the vehicle to close the trunk. As I reached up to pull the lid down I couldn't believe my eyes—there was a handgun lying in plain view right in the middle of the trunk. I shouted, "Mohaska!" to Jeff, and we pulled the guy out of the car and handcuffed him. The look on his face was like, *Shit, I forgot all about that shit.* I couldn't help but wonder if he knew how much he had fucked himself the minute he accidentally hit that trunk-release button.

We brought him into the Four-Seven Precinct for arrest processing. We started filling out the paperwork when he suddenly said, "Can I talk to you guys?"

We put down our pens and pulled our chairs up to his cell. He told us he knew a guy who had sixteen guns in his apartment. We were like, "Really? Did you see them? How do you know this guy? Why are you telling us this shit?"

He then explained that this would be his third felony arrest, and if he got convicted, he would be going away for a long time. We now knew where he was going with this: He was hoping that if he gave us good information, he would get "court consideration" so we listened. Based on our training and experience from interviewing so many suspects throughout the years, we determined that this guy's information was probably legitimate.

When we got down to the Bronx DA's Office, we spoke to the ADA and explained to her what we had. After interviewing the guy herself, she, in turn, found him and his information to be credible. We were then directed to bring him before a judge, where he would be sworn in as a "C.I."(confidential informant). We were issued a search warrant for the address that our C.I. had supplied, along with the names of the suspects he identified who resided there. Jeff and I had been down this road with countless search and arrest warrants before, so we remained cautious that it all might turn out to be nothing—just another desperate perp's attempt to forestall the inevitable. Nonetheless, the next night, warrant in hand we hit the place.

We started searching, and sure enough, we were finding guns all over the place. This guy's information turned out to be right on the money; we recovered sixteen guns—handguns, rifles, ammunition, and even one of the suspects named in the warrant. The search warrant had been successful. The guy had come through for us and himself.

We never did find out if he received the court consideration he requested, but we found ourselves hoping that he did. He had done the right thing, as right a thing as he could have done given his circumstances, which could be a double-edged sword for him. If the guys he gave up were to find out he had given us the information, it wouldn't go well for him. And all because he pushed the wrong button.

46

YOU GOT ME

My partner Jeff and I were assigned to the 114th Precinct doing a 2130-by-0605 tour when Central came over the radio with a "shots-fired" job, coming from the apartment buildings located in the vicinity of Twenty-First Avenue and Forty-Ninth Street in Queens. Street Crime didn't normally respond to radio runs, but we started rolling over to the general vicinity anyway. One of our Street Crime sergeants had already responded and confirmed over the air that someone had been shot at the location and was "D.O.A." (dead on arrival). There were apparently no witnesses and, therefore, no description of the shooter.

The streets were pretty empty that night. We decided to pull over to the curb directly across the street from the DOA's apartment complex and monitor the radio for further information. I saw a male Hispanic cross the street to the Mobile Gas Station at Northern Boulevard and Woodside Avenue. Jeff and I watched him approach a livery cab driver who was gassing up. He had a brief conversation with the cabbie while the cabbie finished pumping gas, and then he got into the backseat of the cab and they pulled out of the gas station. Jeff and I exchanged looks, and without saying a word to each other, we pulled out and started following them. I threw the red light up on the dashboard, and we pulled the cab over. I approached the driver's side, and Jeff went to the right-rear passenger side of the vehicle, pulling open the rear passenger side door.

Suddenly the passenger blurted out, "Okay, you got me. He hurt bad?"

"What are you talking about?" Jeff asked.

"I shot my brother," he replied.

We pulled him from the rear seat of the cab, handcuffed him, patted him down for weapons, and put him in the back of our vehicle. We radioed our sergeant and told him what we had. He responded to our location, and we waited together for detectives from the squad to arrive. It was another one of those situations where because we were always watching people and paying close attention to what was happening around us, we were able to discern when something seemed a little off or out of place. Someone had approached a cabbie in an otherwise empty gas station in the predawn hours when there was no one else on the street and asked for a ride, with no other open stores or bars or clubs. *Where did he come from and where was he headed?* The circumstances seemed unusual to us—something didn't fit. It piqued our curiosity and had us looking a little more closely. The shooter didn't have any blood on him; he wasn't in possession of any weapons, and there were no witnesses to him shooting his own brother, so if he hadn't made a *spontaneous utterance* confessing to the crime when Jeff pulled open the door to the cab, we would have probably let him go on his way.

While we awaited the arrival of the squad, we decided to question the guy to try to get him to tell us where the weapon was. At first he was reluctant to talk, but as time went on Jeff established a good dialogue with him, explaining the importance and urgency of recovering the weapon (which happened to be a shotgun) before some kids could find it and get hurt. He was starting to come around to our way of thinking when suddenly, a detective from the squad showed up. Without a word, he jumped into the backseat of our car, sliding in next to the perp.

There was a momentary silence until the detective said to us, "Hey, I think your sergeant is looking for you."

Simultaneously, we both turned to look in the general direction of our sergeant when we suddenly heard a resounding *crack*, like the sound of someone being slapped across the face. The next thing we heard was our perp saying, "I want my lawyer." And he never said another word after that.

We had been so close to recovering the murder weapon, but within seconds this (apparently drunken) asshole detective ruined everything. The squad took the arrest, so we never did find out if they ever found the shotgun or if the case actually went to trial. I'm guessing that if the guy was hard-core enough to kill his own brother, there was no amount of slaps in the face that were going to convince him to give up the location of the murder weapon he used to do it.

47

I was assigned to drive the sergeant on the overnight tour. We turned out of Street Crime Base and headed for the Four-Six Precinct in the Bronx. We pulled over to the curb to drink our coffee (minus the doughnuts), relaxing for a few minutes but at the same time knowing that a "shots fired" or a pursuit could come over the radio at any time. Being the ever-vigilant cop that I had become, I was drinking my coffee "keeping always on the alert and observing everything that takes place within sight or hearing" (which was part of the *Second General Order of the Marine Corps*).

I turned my head to the right and could actually see in the right side-view mirror several male blacks and Hispanics standing in front of a garage engaged in conversation with two middle-aged male whites. This did not strike me as your usual evening gathering in this neighborhood, so I continued to watch them through the mirror, trying to figure out why this mixed bag had come together and what they could possibly be discussing. Suddenly I saw one of the males hand off what appeared to be a handgun to one of the

149

two male whites. Now it all made sense; the white guys were in the 'hood to buy a gun.

The sergeant had been dozing off when I went on the radio to try to raise a nearby Street Crime unit for backup. Bobby, who happened to be working with my regular partner Wayne, answered up, so I asked them to "10-85" us at our location. I told them we might have something going on. The sergeant roused to ask what was happening, though he had always trusted our instincts whenever it came to a situation that required investigating.

Once the other team arrived on the scene, we pulled up on the guys to question and frisk them for safety reasons, and to my dismay no one was "holding" (carrying a gun). Had my eyes deceived me? I really thought that I had seen the exchange of a firearm between them. I had seen the white guys go back to their car that was parked nearby, so I decided to search the car and—*bingo*—I recovered a semiautomatic handgun from inside their vehicle. Since both of the white guys had been in the vehicle at different times, I placed them both under arrest for possession of the loaded firearm.

We removed both of them to the Four-Six Precinct. We started the paperwork and then one of guys tried pulling the "Italian nationality card", suggesting that since he was *Italian* and I was *Italian*, there must be *something* we could do about the arrest. I looked at him, smiled, and shook my head. Crime knows no nationality, no race, no ethnicity, no gender, no color, and no creed. It is whatever you can see in the side-view mirror.

48

The things I've seen would make most people cringe
Unshakable images make you want to go out on a binge
I've seen people shot for no reason at all
For initiation into a gang or else they themselves will fall.

Maiming and robbing in the name of their colors
All to gain the respect of their newfound brothers
I've seen innocent victims just trying to live their lives
Who will never get to see their own children thrive.

I've seen so much hate for the police, for us all
From the Bronx to Brooklyn and inside City Hall
Laws that were written so many years ago
Now forsaken for whichever way the wind happens to blow.

Elected officials with unqualified pasts
Permitting violence to reign, and it threatens to last.
They cite some ludicrous policy of the day
That forces police to hold back and get out of the way.

Our cops need to be respected and empowered to facedown crime
To bring our city back to the people one street at a time.
Allegiance to the largest police department in the world they swore
Make them proud to wear the uniform once more.

49

What's Going On

I walk around today, looking at cops—cops whose faces are buried in their cell phones. I want to shout at them: Why aren't you paying attention? Don't you realize what can happen to you? There are people out there who hate your guts—they want to see you dead. You need to stay sharp; it doesn't matter which command you are assigned to. There are cop-hating, mentally-ill, antipolice, cell-phone-videoing, lawless individuals out there on the street who want to do you harm. Stay alert while you're sitting in your patrol car, shooting the shit with your partner. There are hundreds of eyes on you, always watching you. These are the people who love to see police officers get into confrontations with individuals; in fact, they live for it. This is the world we live in today; people would rather pull out their cell phones and start recording than jump in to try to help you—the cop rolling around on the ground with some asshole trying to take your gun away.

I have spoken to a lot of cops, and many of them say the same thing—that the days of stopping someone because you *suspected* they had a weapon are over. While it's true enough that they did away with *stop, question, and frisk*, did that mean that a police officer is now expected to give up his or her life rather than search a person whom, based on their training and experience, they reasonably believe is carrying a firearm? I don't think so. The powers that be have the cops of today second-guessing themselves. Instead of investigating and searching, they want cops to "take a breath and close their eyes for a moment." Close your eyes for a moment on the street, and you may never be able to open them again.

Cops backing up as demonstrators approach, closing the space between them, people screaming in the cops' faces, nose-to-nose, cursing and spitting. The videos of such behaviors going viral … Never mind the lack of respect for authority. Where are the tactics? If as a cop, you hesitate when you should be taking action in a reasonable capacity as a law-enforcement officer, *you will die*. Your goal is to *stay alive*. You have a difficult, dangerous job, but you have a family, and they love and depend on you. And the most important part of your job is to be able to go home at the end of your tour.

Your life impacts so many others. When you're out there on the street, stay alert. Know the law. Use good tactics. Protect yourself. And when you observe someone breaking the law, do what you were trained to do. Stop worrying about getting sued. Don't let people intimidate you or get too close to you. Focus on protecting yourself, your partners, and the innocent people around you. You have earned the right to wear the uniform of the New York City Police Department. Wear it proudly. Wear it in a way that lets them know who is in charge. And that's *you*.

50

I wrote about the Sixth Precinct because it was my first permanent command. The Sixth Precinct was where I really learned how to be a cop, from my earliest days walking a foot post to getting assigned to a steady sector car and eventually working my way up to the Anticrime Unit. In the Sixth Precinct I got to be partners with my best friend, Les. The Sixth Precinct was where I learned how to watch people, observe behaviors, ask the right questions, trust my instincts, and hone my skills. The Sixth Precinct was where I was able to reach that pivotal point in my career where I knew I was ready for more—to be more and to do more. I was prepared for what would prove to be the most challenging and gratifying time of my career.

Most of my stories center on my time in the Street Crime Unit because it was the most exciting and rewarding time of my twenty years in the New York City Police Department. In Street Crime I was proud to get to work with the best of the best cops the NYPD had to offer. We were there because we had earned the right to be there, and we continued to prove ourselves on the streets night after night in some of the worst precincts in the city. We were street-smart and fearless, sharp and proactive. We got down and dirty, scouring the streets each night looking for people with guns, and we wouldn't go end of tour until we got them. There are so many more stories—car chases, robberies, burglaries, larcenies, violent disputes, drug collars—I couldn't possibly include them all. I made more than a thousand arrests and was partner to hundreds more.

I've been retired for thirteen years now, and whenever I talk about the job, it is always the Street Crime stories I tell, almost forgetting that I was ever assigned to Citywide Gang or Narcotics Units. There will never be another time, and there will never be another unit in the NYPD like Street Crime again. It is etched in the hearts and minds of all the cops who passed through the Street Crime doors.

I think back to the very first collar I made in the Sixty-Seventh Precinct. I remember how overwhelmed I had felt, not knowing exactly what paperwork had to be done and wanting to make sure I did everything right. I was so grateful when that seasoned cop with the rack of medals extending over his shoulder swooped in and starting thrusting forms at me and telling me what notifications had to be made. After that day, I promised myself that I would become *that* cop—the cop who knew the job inside and out, the cop who was able to answer other cops' questions, the cop who worked in every precinct and command in the city. I became that cop. And a whole lot more.

NYPD Jargon

bag of shit. An incident wherein what transpired and/or the identity of the witnesses/complainant cannot be determined; no one can be ID'd

to bang in. Police officer taking off or calling out sick without advance notice

Basement Police. NYC Transit Police

Central. 911 dispatcher who contacts police officers on post and in sector cars via radio transmission to give them their assignments

collar. Arrest

Country Club. A precinct in a relatively low-crime, well-to-do neighborhood

DOA (dead on arrival). A deceased individual discovered by police upon arrival at the scene

detail. An assignment taking place outside of the regular precinct/command (parade, demonstration, marathon, riot, etc.)

drop a dime (or rat out). One police officer informing on another

empty suit (or zero). A police officer who does the bare minimum; never works overtime, makes arrests, or helps a fellow officer

flip-flop (or turn-around). Alternating day and evening tours consecutively

floater. Dead human body pulled from a body of water

flute. Plastic Coca-Cola cup containing soda and alcohol

flying. Temporary reassignment to a precinct or command outside of the officer's permanent

foot post. A police officer assigned to a post on foot for the tour

a good cop. Never gets cold, wet, or hungry, because he or she knows how to stay out of the elements and knows the best places to eat at the best prices

ground ball. An arrest where everything seems to fall into place easily—perps, witnesses, evidence, and overtime

gun-heavy. A police officer who always stands around with his or her hand on his or her weapon

hair-bag. A cop who gives the outward appearance of having been there, done that, and knows everything there is to know about policing

the Heave. Police officer sleeping quarters (dorm) in the precinct

heavy house. Precinct with extremely high amount of crime

the Hole. Subway

home run. High-profile, highly publicized arrest of a perp wanted for a pattern of robberies or homicide

hook. A high-placed connection within the police department who can get things done (transfers, etc.)

Hotel Security. NYC Housing Police

in the bag. Working in uniform

jammed up. Police officer in trouble for doing something wrong

a job. Radio run from Central or other assignment (like precinct or pickup)

kid. Nickname for a police officer, no matter what age, who has less experience than the older cop calling him or her that

launched. A cop immediately and permanently transferred from his or her precinct because of an incident (a.k.a. administrative transfer)

likely. An individual so severely injured that risk of death is imminent

looking. When a police officer is actively searching for an arrest

lost time. A police officer's request to use banked time to take a few hours off his or her assigned tour

muster (or mustering). Police personnel reporting for a detail outside their regular precinct where they are accounted for, inspected, and assigned to a post

new jack. A police officer newly assigned to a precinct

off-limits location. A business suspected of providing free or discounted meals or services to cops; monitored by Internal Affairs Bureau (IAB)

on-the-job. A city or state agency police officer (most commonly, NYPD)

on-the-arm. Free

perp (or bad guy). Suspect

precinct condition. A low-level misdemeanor charge ineligible for a desk appearance ticket (DAT) because it happened too often in that precinct

put it over. A police officer transmitting descriptions, past crimes, or pursuits via radio to the central dispatcher

RMP. Radio motor patrol (marked police) car

roll call. Assembly of police officers at the beginning of each tour where they would be inspected and receive their assignments

a scratch. Supervisor's signature in a police officer's memo book to indicate that he or she checked in on that police officer

shaky. Any uniformed member of the police department of any rank who lacked confidence and appeared unable to make a decision

shitcan. Get rid of; make disappear

shoo-fly. Duty captain or above who conducts unannounced inspections (visits) to precincts and commands within a division

skell. Nasty, dirty, smelly person; usually someone living on the street (a.k.a. homeless)

the Squad. Detectives in the precinct

toe (or 95) tag. An identification tag placed on the big toe of the deceased

took a collar. A police officer made an arrest

whacking it up. Two or more police officers sharing the same post/assignment taking turns standing post and taking breaks

wood shampoo. To get hit in the head with a nightstick

Printed in the United States
By Bookmasters